Gou...

THE CAROLINAS

ROAD ATLAS

AND VISITOR'S GUIDE

TEXT: MARY T. MULKERIN / DESIGN: EDWARD P. O'DELL

Table of Contents

H.M. Gousha
A Paramount Communications Company

The Carolinas

North Carolina

Capital...Raleigh
Nickname...................................Tar Heel State
Motto......................................*Esse Quam Videri*
    (To Be Rather Than To Seem)
Bird...Cardinal
Tree..Pine
Flower ....American dogwood

South Carolina

Capital..Columbia
Nickname ....Palmetto State
Motto ....*Dum Spiro Spero*
    (While I Breathe, I Hope)
Bird...Carolina wren
Tree...Palmetto
Flower ....Carolina yellow jessamine

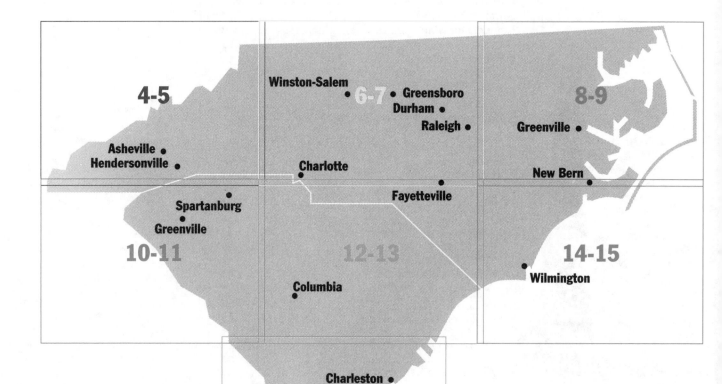

4-5

Winston-Salem • **6-7** • **Greensboro**
Durham •
Raleigh •

8-9

Greenville •

Asheville •
Hendersonville •

Charlotte •

New Bern •

Spartanburg •

Greenville •

10-11

Fayetteville •

12-13

14-15

Wilmington •

Columbia •

Charleston •

16-17

KEY TO MAP PAGES

To find detailed road map
of area outlined, turn to
page numbers indicated.

CAROLINAS

How to Read Your Atlas Maps

SCALE IN MILES AND KILOMETERS

ONE INCH 13 MILES   0   5   10   20

ONE INCH 22 KILOMETERS   0   5   10   20   32

HIGHWAY MARKERS

INTERSTATE (85)   UNITED STATES (64)   STATE (73)

ROAD CLASSIFICATIONS

CONTROLLED ACCESS HIGHWAYS   Divided **33** Undivided
Interstate interchange numbers are mileposts.

       Interchanges

TOLL HIGHWAYS

OTHER DIVIDED HIGHWAYS

PRINCIPAL THROUGH HIGHWAYS   Paved

OTHER THROUGH HIGHWAYS   Paved

CONNECTING HIGHWAYS   Paved   Gravel

LOCAL ROADS In unfamiliar areas inquire locally   Paved   Gravel   Dirt
before using these roads

MILEAGES

LONG DISTANCE MILEAGES SHOWN IN RED

MILEAGE BETWEEN TOWNS AND JUNCTIONS   3 ⁄ 4   MILEAGE BETWEEN DOTS   35

ONE MILE EQUALS 1.6 KILOMETERS   ONE KILOMETER EQUALS .6 MILES

SPECIAL FEATURES

STATE PARKS
With Campsites ▲ Without Campsites △

RECREATION AREAS
With Campsites ▲ Without Campsites △

SELECTED REST AREAS
With Toilets ✕ Without Toilets ✕

TOURIST INFORMATION   ✪

SCHEDULED AIRLINE STOPS ✈

MILITARY AIRPORTS ✈

OTHER AIRPORTS ✈

BOAT RAMPS

SKI AREAS

POINTS OF INTEREST ✕

COUNTY LINES

POPULATION SYMBOLS

⊛ State Capital   ⊗ 2,500 to 5,000   ◻ 25,000 to 50,000

○ Under 1,000   ◉ 5,000 to 10,000   ◼ 50,000 to 100,000

◎ 1,000 to 2,500   ◉ 10,000 to 25,000   ◼ 100,000 and over

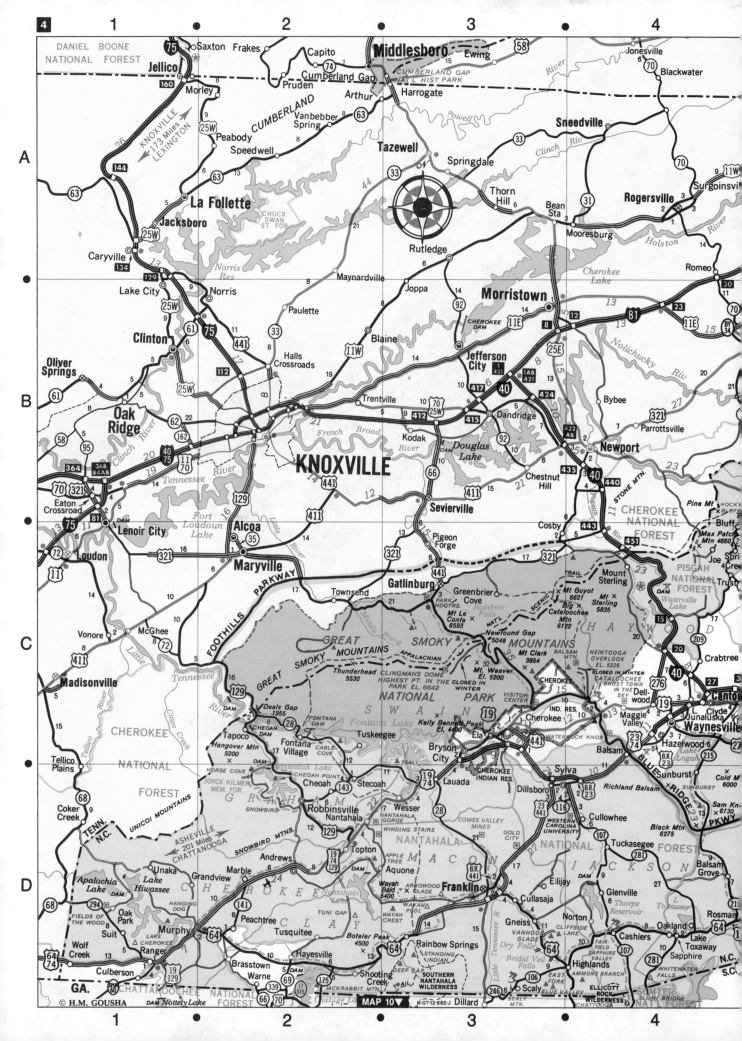

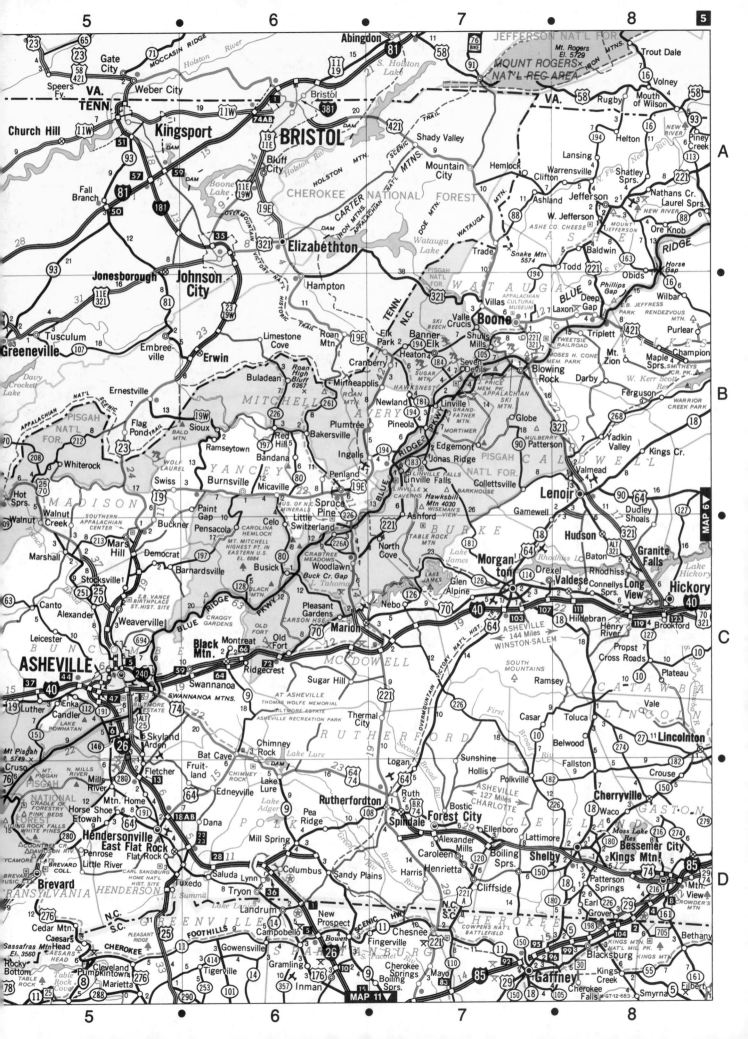

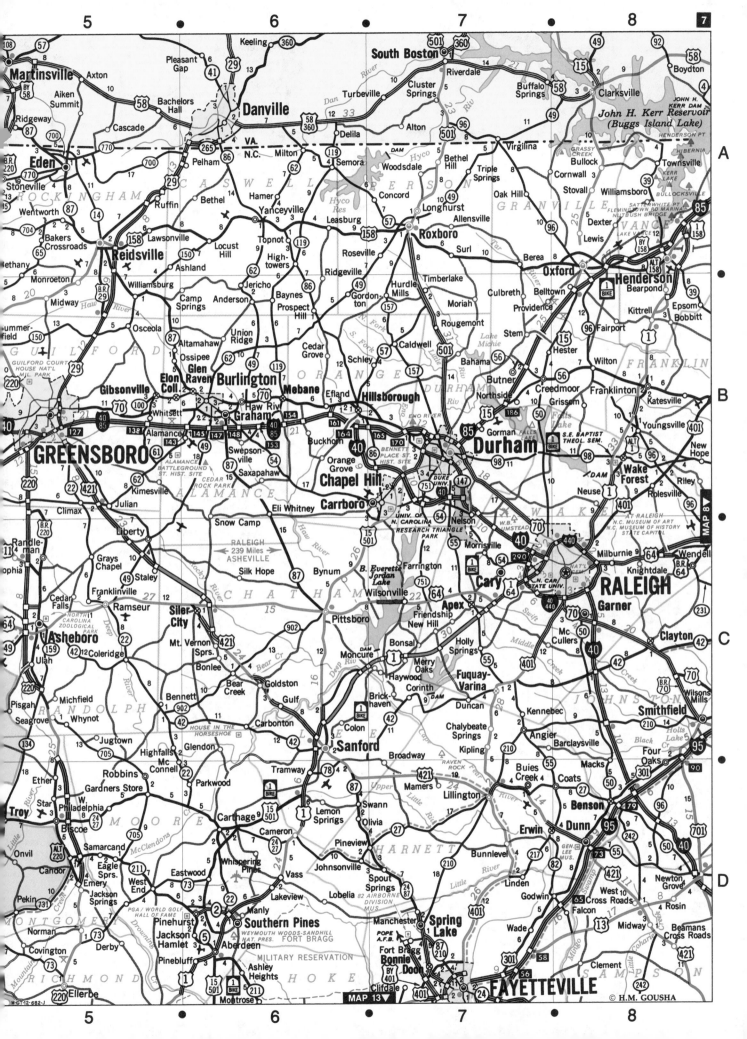

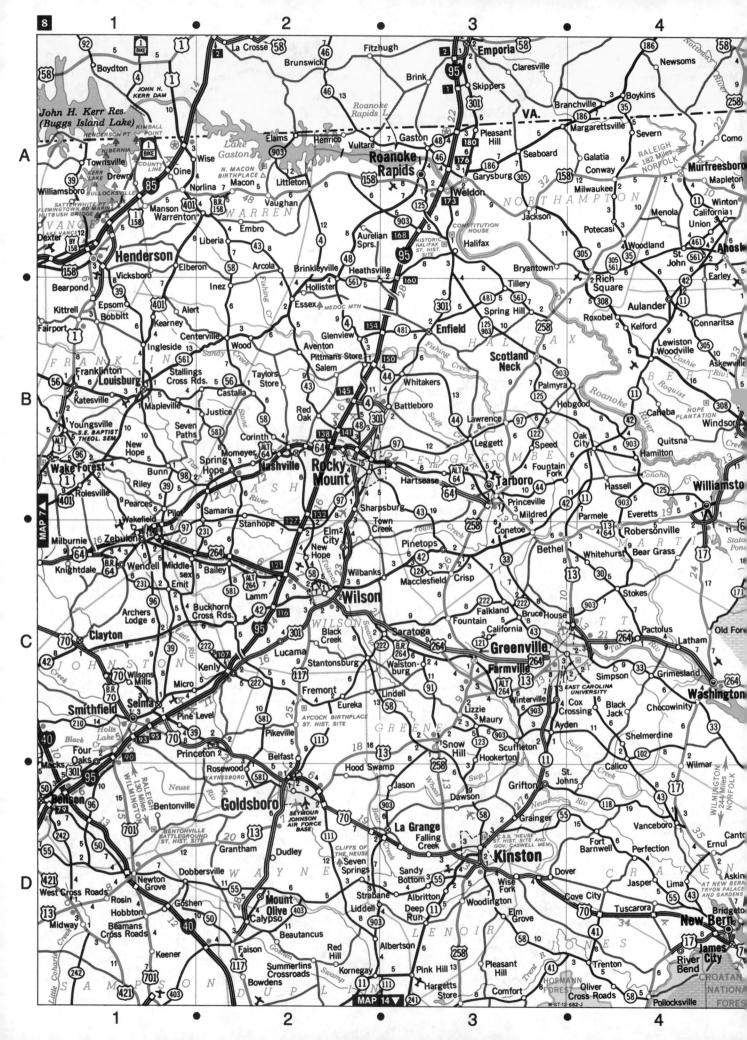

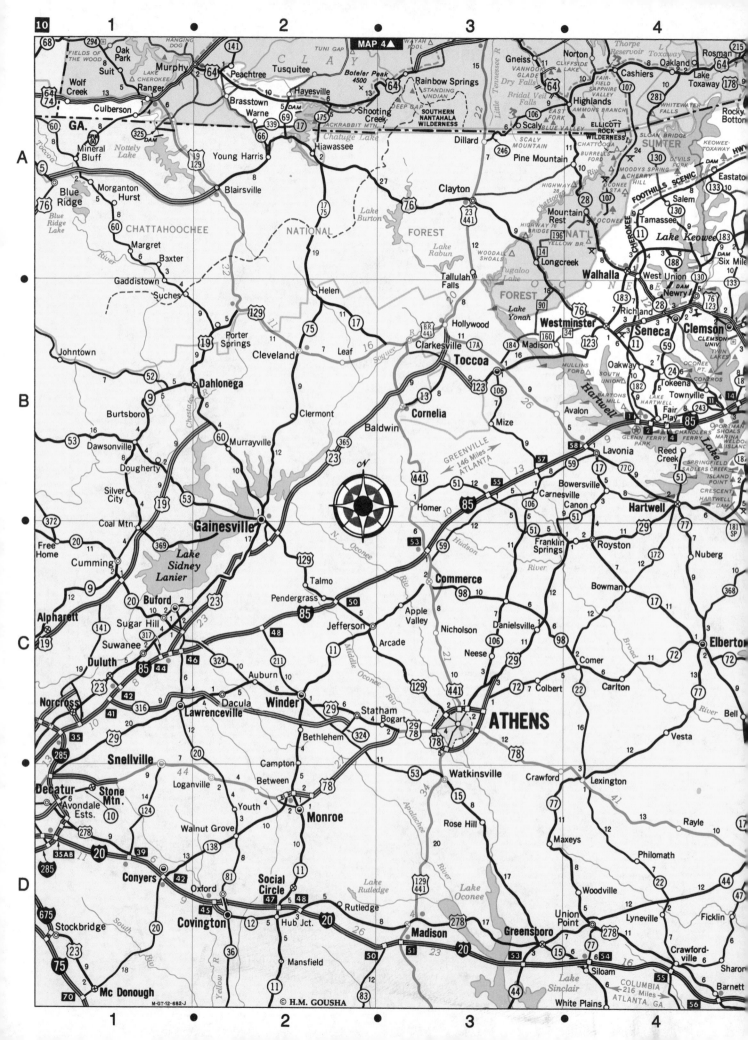

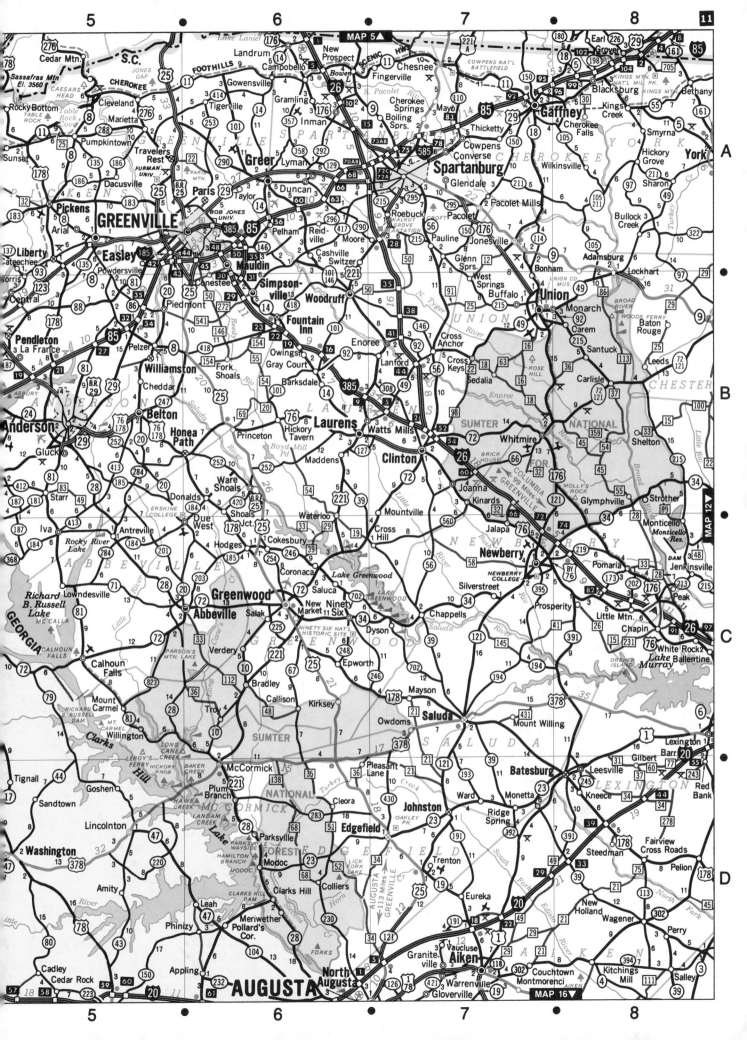

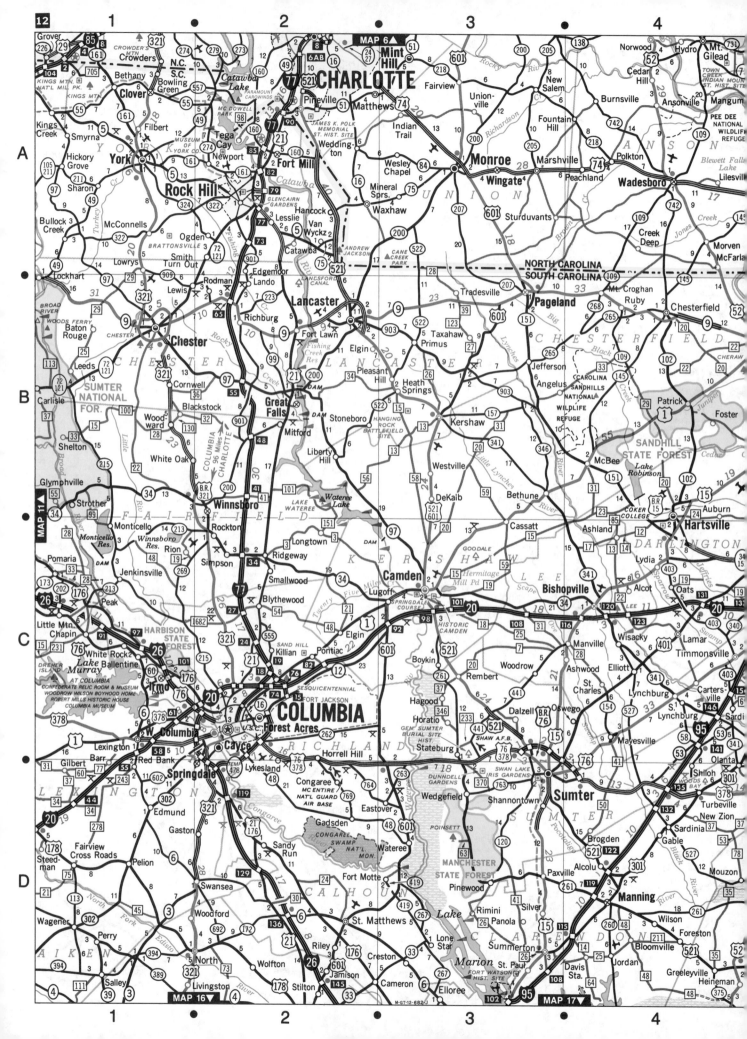

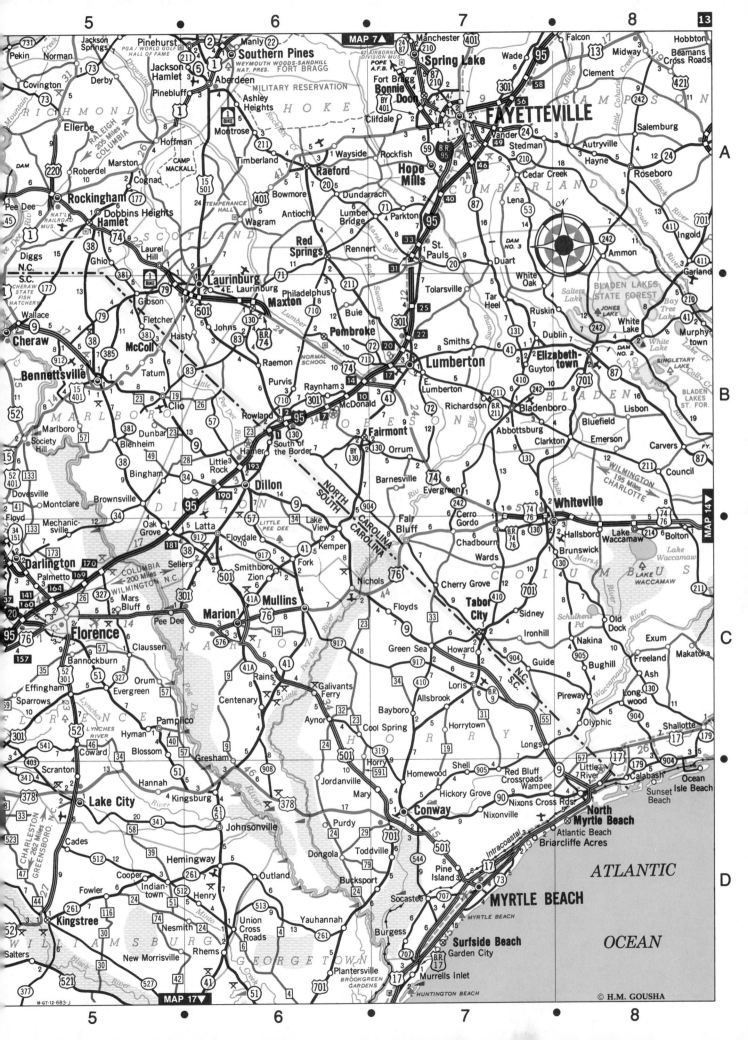

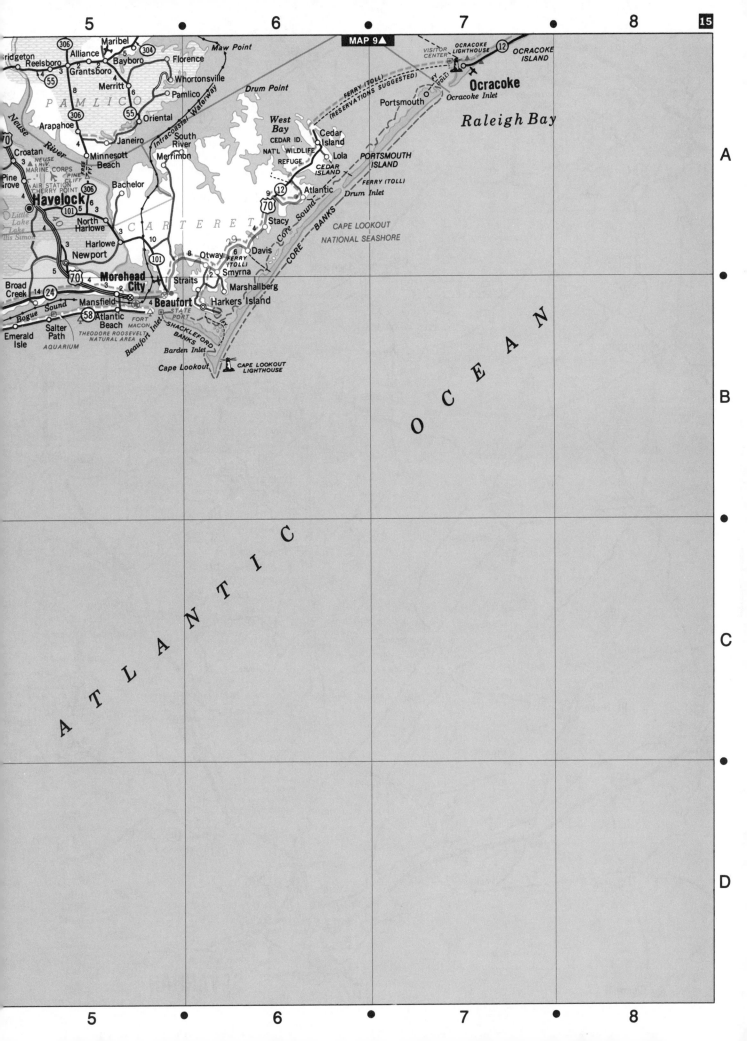

5   6   7   8

MAP 9 ▲

OCRACOKE LIGHTHOUSE
VISITOR CENTER
OCRACOKE ISLAND
12
Ocracoke
Ocracoke Inlet

306 Maribel
Alliance
Bridgeton Reelsboro 304 Bayboro Florence
55 Grantsboro Maw Point
Merritt Whortonsville
8 55 Pamlico
PAMLICO Oriental Drum Point Portsmouth
306 Arapahoe West Bay *Raleigh Bay*
Neuse River Janeiro CEDAR ID. Cedar Island
70 Croatan South Merrimon NAT'L WILDLIFE Lola PORTSMOUTH ISLAND
Minnesott River REFUGE CEDAR ISLAND
3 Beach ISLAND FERRY (TOLL)
Pine NEUSE I RIV Bachelor 9 12 Atlantic Drum Inlet
Grove MARINE CORPS Atlantic CAPE LOOKOUT
AIR STATION 306 70 NATIONAL SEASHORE
Havelock CHERRY POINT Stacy
101 North 3 Core Sound CORE BANKS
Little Harlowe 10 29
Lake Harlowe 8 Otway 6 Davis
Illis Simon Newport 101 FERRY
5 70 Straits Smyrna (TOLL)
Broad 24 Morehead 3 2 Marshallberg
Creek 14 City Beaufort Harkers Island
Mansfield STATE
Bogue Sound 58 Atlantic FORT PORT
Emerald Salter Beach MACON SHACKLEFORD
Isle Path THEODORE ROOSEVELT Beaufort Inlet BANKS
NATURAL AREA Barden Inlet
AQUARIUM Cape Lookout CAPE LOOKOUT LIGHTHOUSE

FERRY (TOLL)
(RESERVATIONS SUGGESTED)
FY (TOLL)

C A R T E R E T

O C E A N

A T L A N T I C

A

B

C

D

5   6   7   8

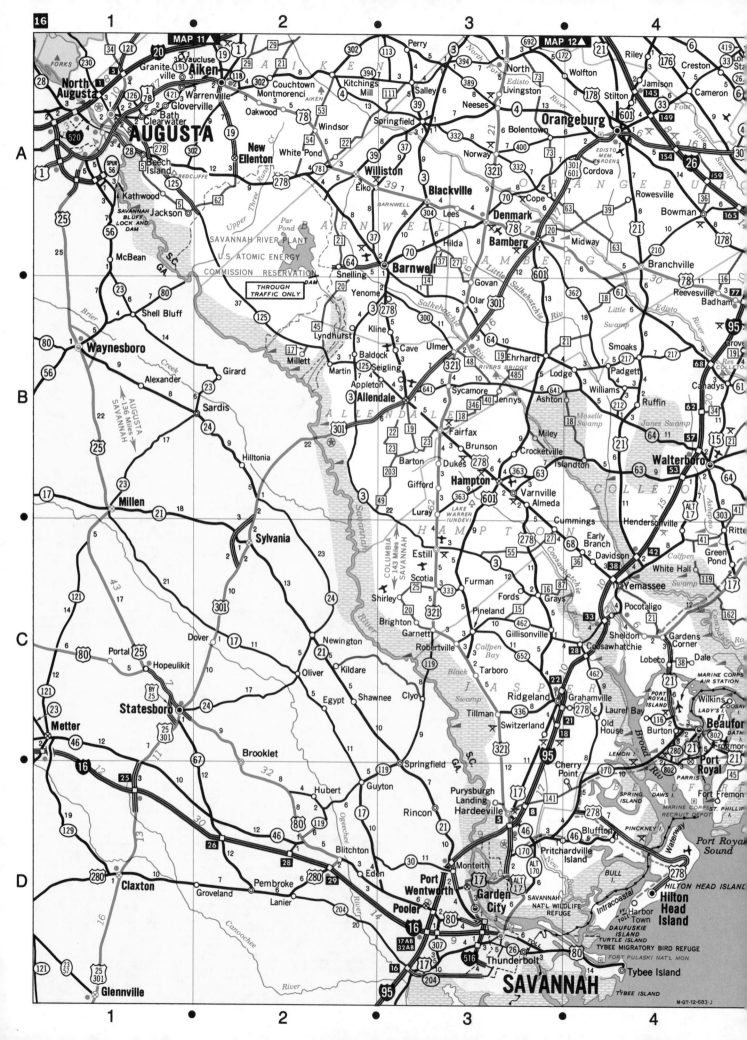

City Maps

ANDERSON-South Carolina

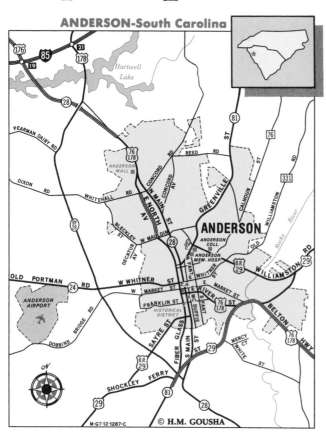

ASHEVILLE-North Carolina

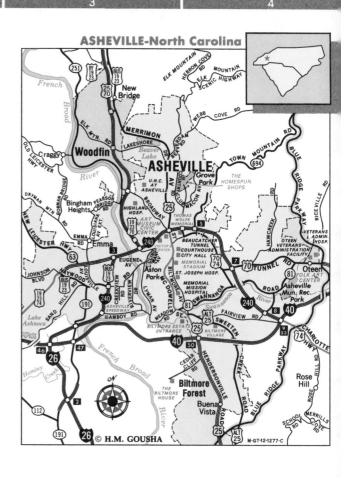

AUGUSTA-AIKEN-South Carolina

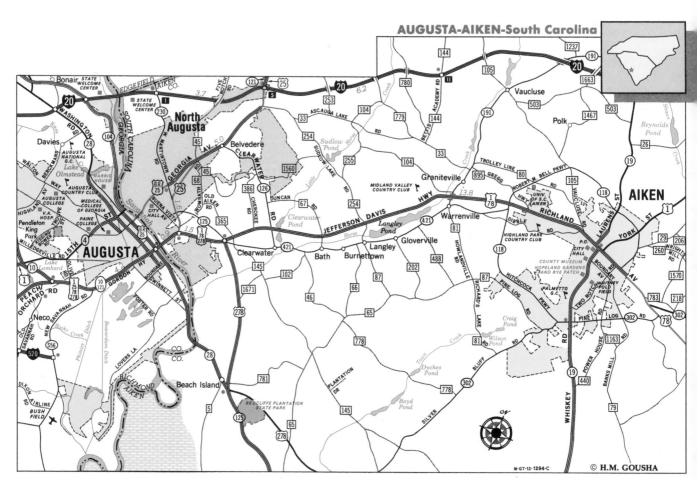

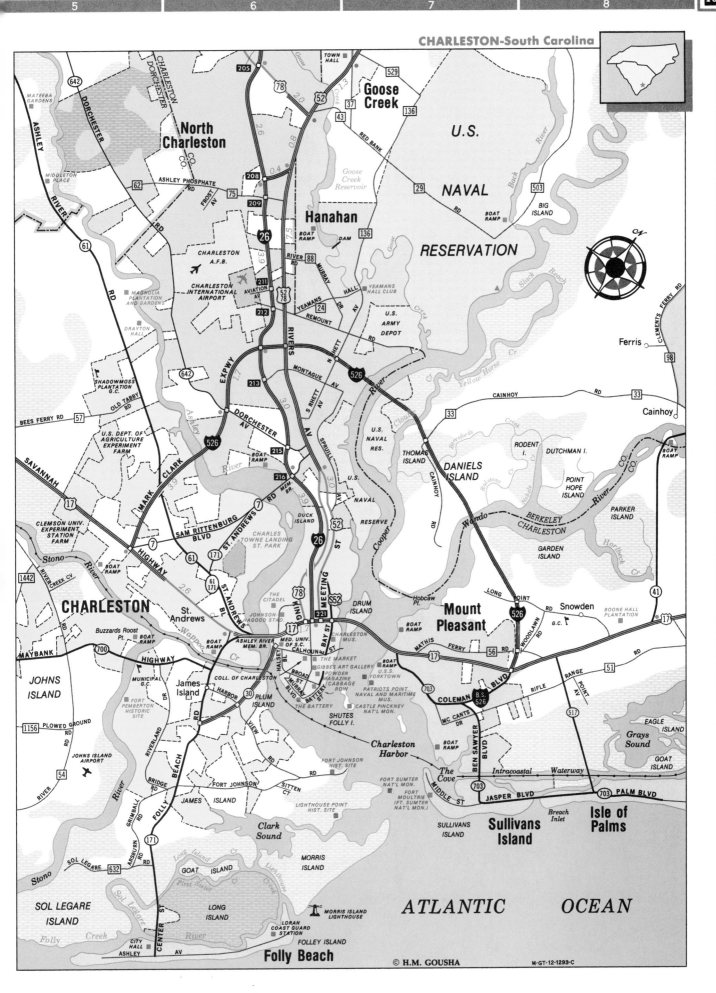

CHARLESTON-South Carolina

© H.M. GOUSHA

M-GT-12-1293-C

1   2   3   4

CHARLOTTE-North Carolina

Pumpkin Center
Denver
150
Triangle
16
Lincolnton
73
Iron Station
High Shoals
321
Alexis
27
Lucia
Lowesville
LINCOLN CO.
GASTON CO.
Stanley
275
273
Dallas
279
321
275
Spencer Mountain
Ranlo
Mount Holly
17
Lowell
14
McAdenville
North Belmont
29 74
85
Cramerton
Belmont
GASTONIA
274
279
273
27
Schiele Museum of Natural History and Planetarium
Belmont Abbey Cathedral
Crowders
Gastonia Municipal Airport
MECKLENBURG GASTON
NORTH CAROLINA
SOUTH CAROLINA
GASTON YORK CO. CO.
Bowling Green
Clover
557
55
321
Catawba Lake
BOAT RAMP
49
MC DOWELL PARK
274
BOAT RAMP
York
49
161
324
Newport
Municipal Airport
161
WINTHROP COLLEGE
322
901
274
GLENCAIRN GARDENS
72 121
82
79
77
Fishing Creek
321
McConnells
324
Ogden
BRATTONSVILLE
ROCK HILL
73
Smith Turn Out
Lowrys
909
72 121
Lewis
909
Rodman
77
Lando
901
223

Lake Norman
COWANS FORD DAM
73
Mountain Island Lake
MOUNTAIN ISLAND DAM
16
LATTA PLACE
FREEDOM DR
LITTLE ROCK RD
32
33
28
Charlotte Douglas Int'l Airport
521
WEST BLVD
CITY 4
160
SHOPTON RD
COLISEUM
49
5
PINEVILLE RD
YORK RD
TYVOLA RD
6.8
3
PARAMOUNT CAROWINDS
INFORMATION CENTER
MECKLENBURG YORK CO. CO.
90
51
Pineville
77
PTL-HERITAGE U.S.A.
21
MECKLENBURG LANCASTER
85
CATAWBA DAM
MUSEUM OF YORK COUNTY
Tega Cay
Wylie Lake
160
Fort Mill
CATAWBA INDIAN RESERVATION
5
Catawba
Van Wyczk
LANCASTER CHESTER
521
LANDSFORD CANAL STATE PARK
200
522

77
115
Davidson
DAVIDSON COLLEGE
21
28
Cornelius
73
23
MC INTYRE HISTORIC SITE
Huntersville
115
SUNSET RD
16 AB RD
GIBBON RD
16
13 AB 38
36
34
85
277
SMITH UNIV.
27
29 74
9
SPIRIT SQUARE
8
TYRON ST
277
NATURE MUSEUM
QUEENS COLLEGE
CITY 4
3.2
GRAHAM ST
39
40
41
TRYON ST
DISCOVERY PLACE
AFRO-AMERICAN CULTURAL CENTER
MINT MUSEUM
CHARLOTTE
HEZEKIAH ALEXANDER HOMESITE
OLD CONCORD RD
GRIER RD
WENDOVER RD
16
RAMA RD
FAIRVIEW RD
SHARON RD
CARMEL RD
SARDIS RD
PROVIDENCE RD
ALBEMARLE RD
24 27
IDLEWILD RD
INDEPENDENCE BLVD
6.8
74
PINEVILLE-MATTHEWS ROAD
Matthews
51
Stallings
MECKLENBURG UNION
Indian Trail
JAMES K. POLK MEMORIAL STATE HISTORICAL SITE
521
MECKLENBURG LANCASTER
16
Weddington
75
Hancock
Waxhaw
ANDREW JACKSON STATE PARK
ANDREW JACKSON BIRTHPLACE
75
UNION CO.
LANCASTER CO.
521

ROWAN CO.
IREDELL CO.
Landis
153
29 601
85
BAKERS MILL PARK
ROWAN CABARRUS
KANNAPOLIS
136
CANNON MILLS VISITOR CENTER
ALT 29
63
55
58
BR 601
CONCORD
85
601
CHARLOTTE MOTOR SPEEDWAY
48
29
51
12
49
UNIV. OF N.C. AT CHARLOTTE
45
43
Harrisburg
CABARRUS MECKLENBURG
HARRISBURG RD
COUNTY
24 27
Wilgrove Air Park
Allen
Wilgrove
51
218
Mint Hill
Mint Hill-Matthews Airport
601
Fairview
9.1
119
Monroe Municipal Airport
Wesley Chapel
84
MONROE
74
75
207
Mineral Springs
CANE CREEK PARK
NORTH CAROLINA
SOUTH CAROLINA

IREDELL MECKLENBURG CO. CO.

ROWAN MECKLENBURG

A B C D E F

M-GT-12-1600-S

© H.M. GOUSHA

COLUMBIA-South Carolina

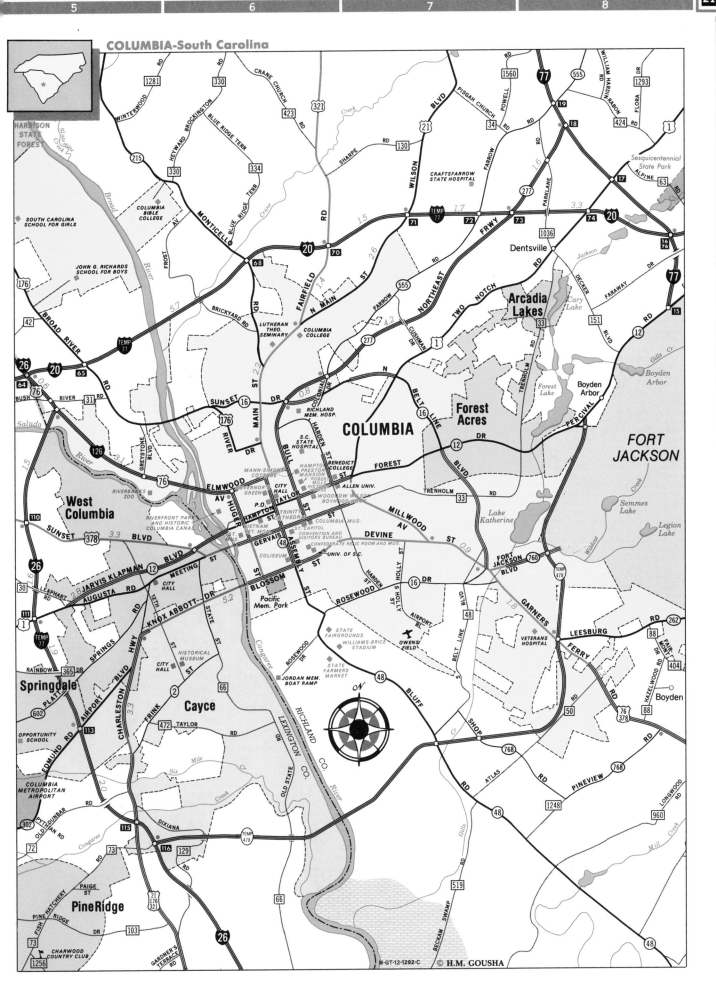

M-GT-12-1292-C © H.M. GOUSHA

FAYETTEVILLE-North Carolina

© H.M. GOUSHA

M-GT-12-1275-C

FLORENCE-South Carolina

© H.M. GOUSHA

M-GT-12-1291-C

GREAT SMOKY MOUNTAINS NATIONAL PARK-North Carolina

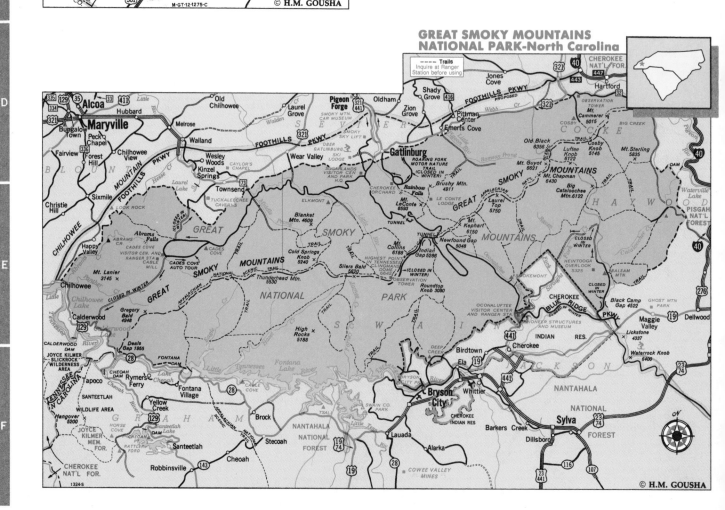

© H.M. GOUSHA

1324-S

THE GRAND STRAND-South Carolina

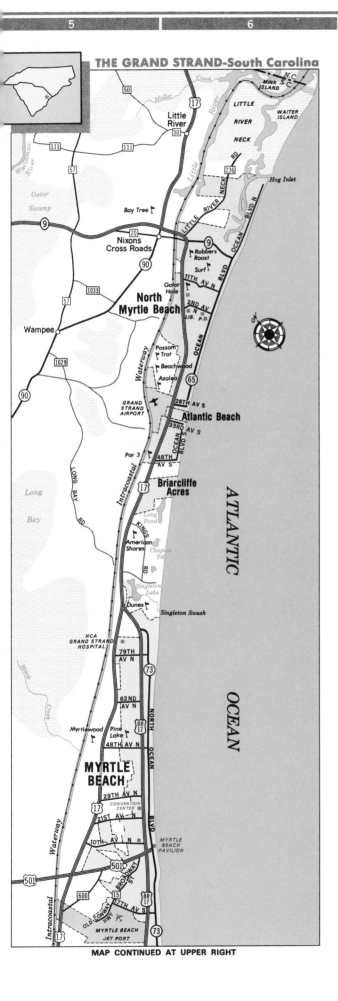

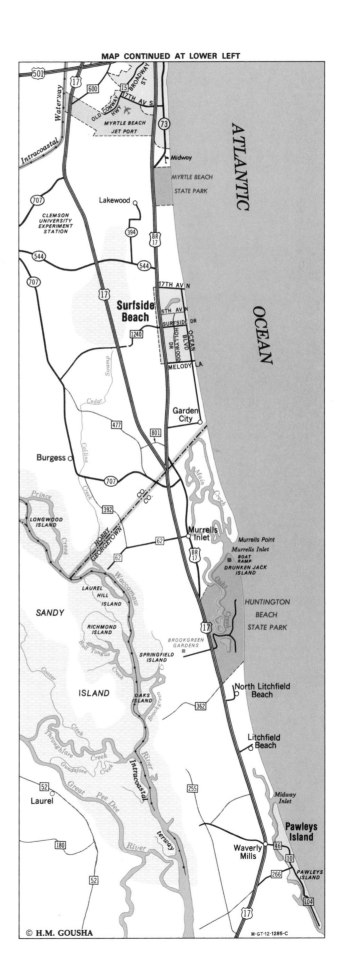

MAP CONTINUED AT LOWER LEFT

MAP CONTINUED AT UPPER RIGHT

© H.M. GOUSHA

M-GT-12-1285-C

GREENVILLE-North Carolina

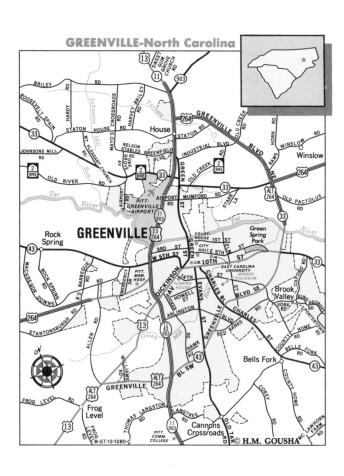

HENDERSONVILLE-North Carolina

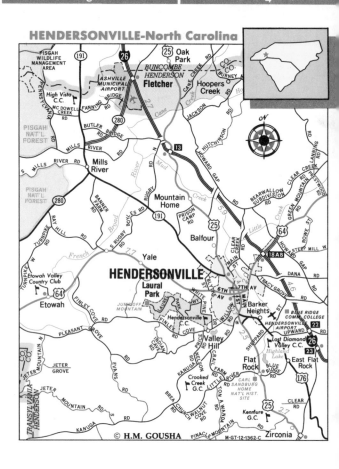

GREENVILLE-South Carolina

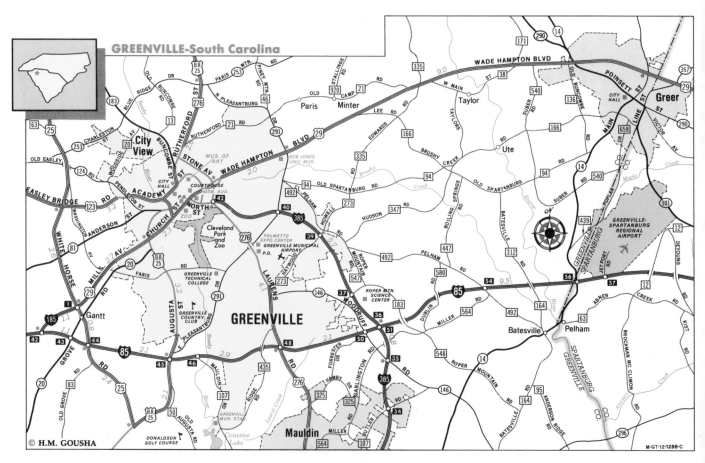

HICKORY-North Carolina

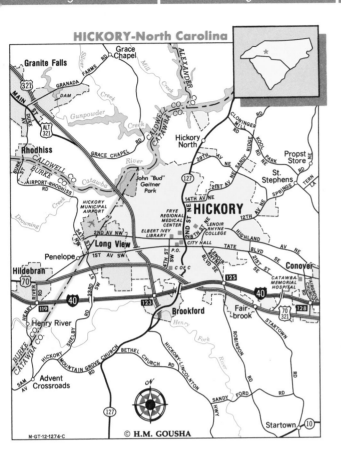

HILTON HEAD ISLAND-South Carolina

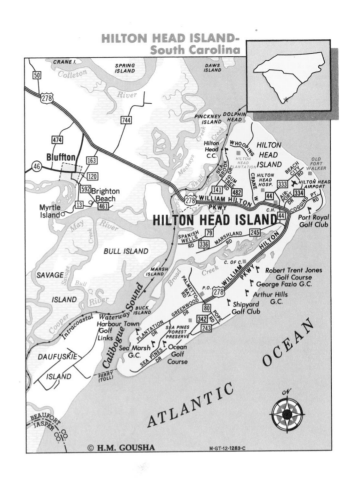

NEW BERN-North Carolina

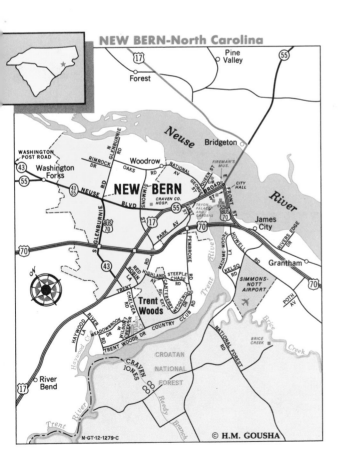

RESEARCH TRIANGLE PARK-North Carolina

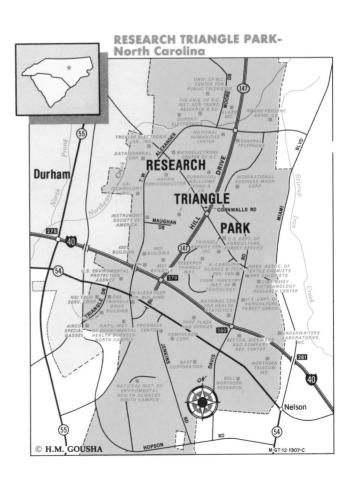

RALEIGH-DURHAM-North Carolina

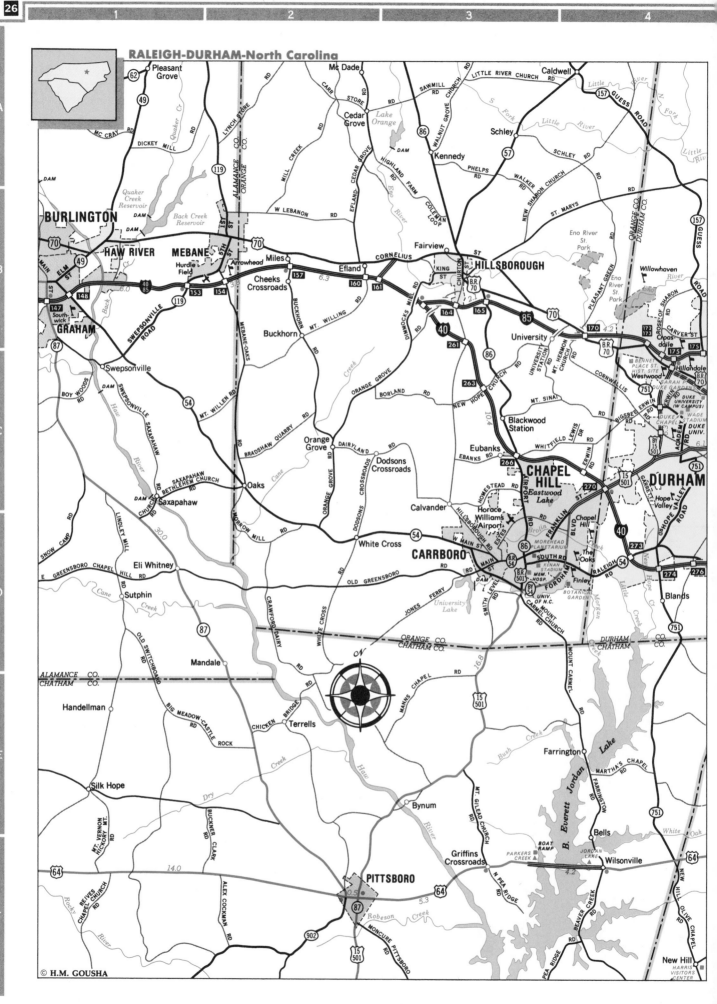

© H.M. GOUSHA

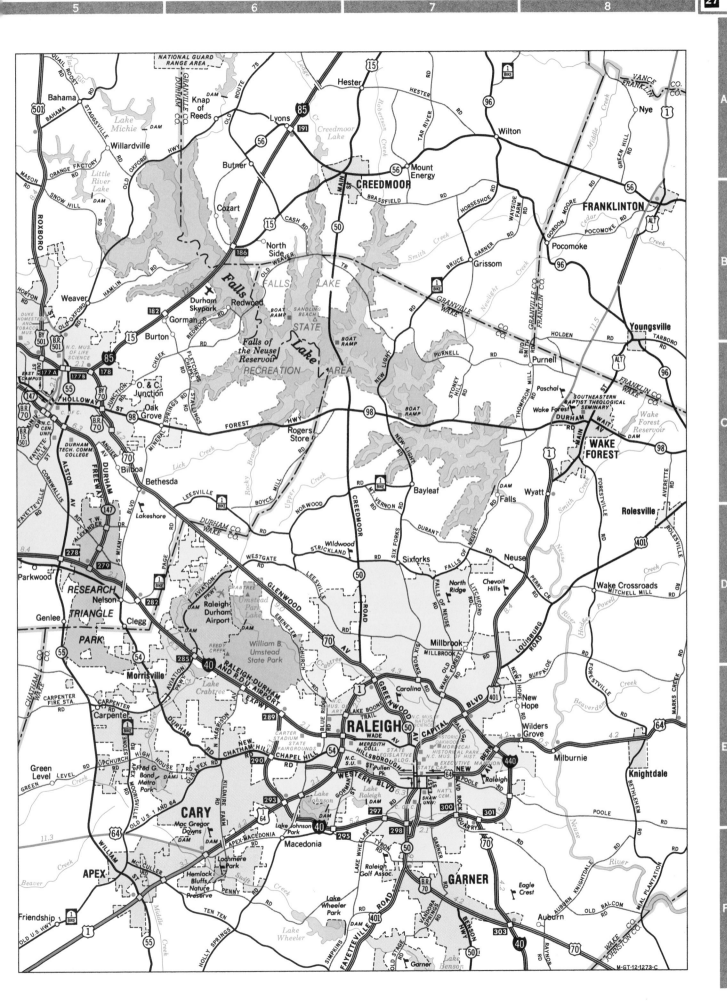

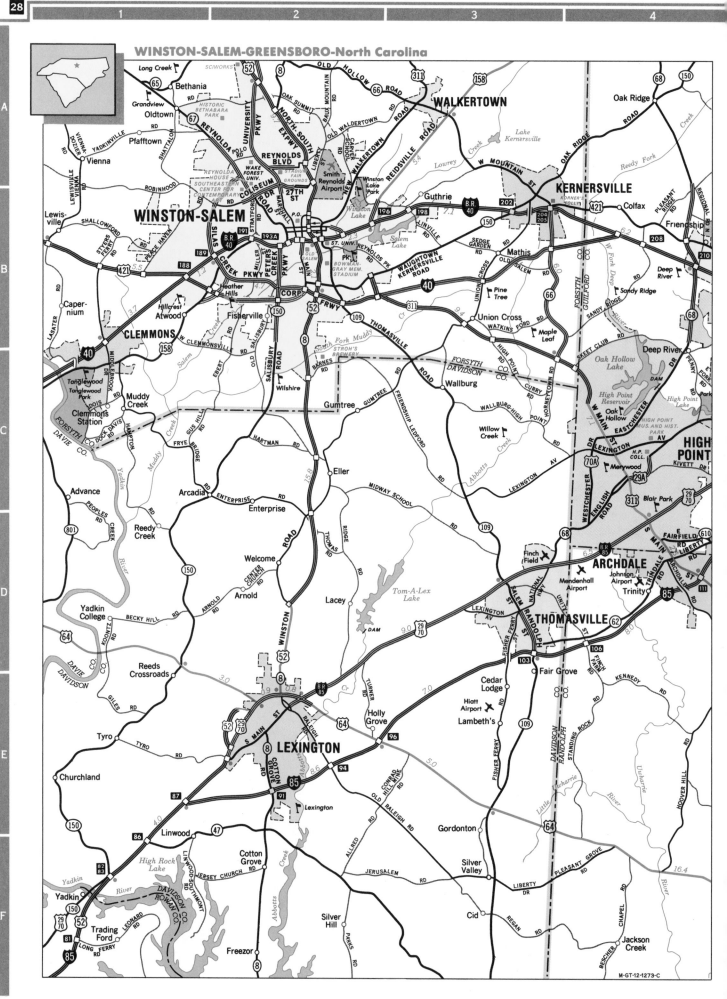

WINSTON-SALEM-GREENSBORO-North Carolina

M-GT-12-1273-C

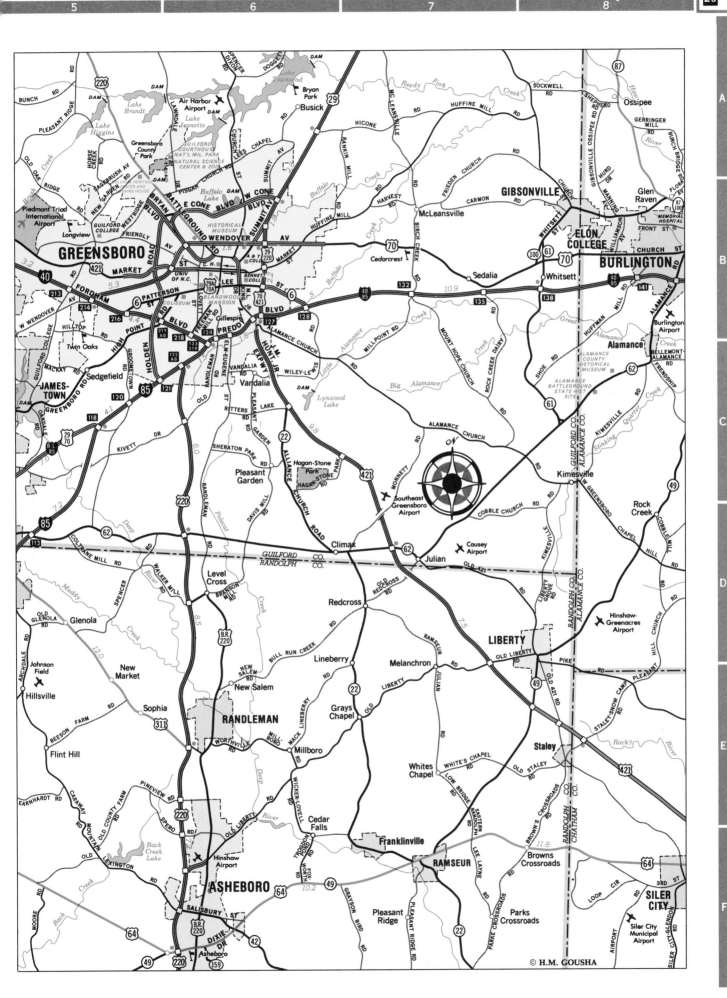

© H.M. GOUSHA

A   B   C   D   E   F

ROCKHILL-South Carolina

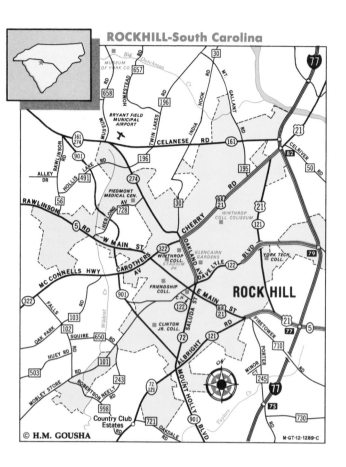

© H.M. GOUSHA

M-GT-12-1289-C

ROCKY MOUNT-North Carolina

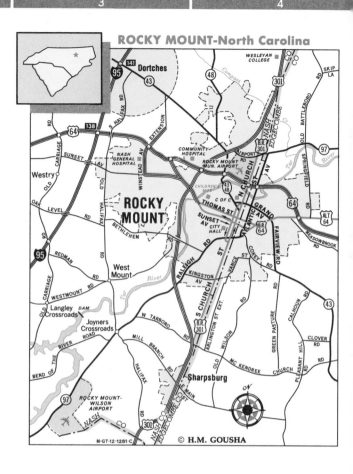

© H.M. GOUSHA

M-GT-12-1281-C

SPARTANBURG-South Carolina

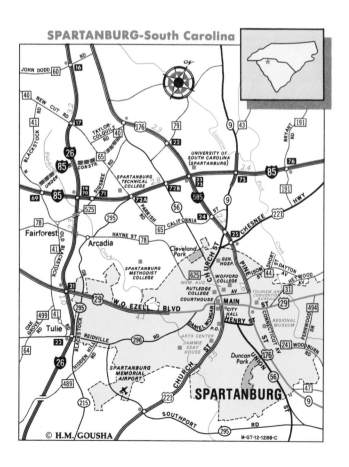

© H.M. GOUSHA

M-GT-12-1288-C

WILMINGTON-North Carolina

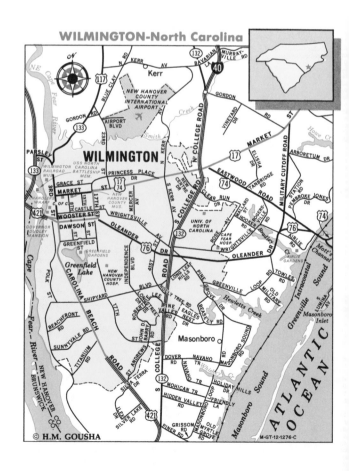

© H.M. GOUSHA

M-GT-12-1276-C

Place ... Population ... Page Grid
Aberdeen ... 2,700 ... 13-A6

NORTH CAROLINA

Pop. (1990) 6,628,637
Area 52,712 Sq. Mi.

COUNTIES

)unty ... County Seat
amance ... Graham
exander ... Taylorsville
leghany ... Sparta
ıson ... Wadesboro
she ... Jefferson
very ... Newland
aufort ... Washington
ertie ... Windsor
ncombie ... Asheville
aden ... Elizabethtown
unswick ... Southport
urke ... Morganton
abarrus ... Concord
aldwell ... Lenoir
amden ... Camden
arteret ... Beaufort
aswell ... Yanceyville
atawba ... Newton
hatham ... Pittsboro
herokee ... Murphy
howan ... Edenton
ay ... Hayesville
eveland ... Shelby
olumbus ... Whiteville
raven ... New Bern
umberland ... Fayetteville
urrituck ... Currituck
are ... Manteo
avidson ... Lexington
avie ... Mocksville
uplin ... Kenansville
urham ... Tarboro
orsyth ... Winston-Salem
anklin ... Louisburg
aston ... Gastonia
ates ... Robbinsville
ranville ... Oxford
reene ... Snow Hill
uilford ... Greensboro
alifax ... Halifax
arnett ... Lillington
aywood ... Waynesville
enderson ... Hendersonville
ertford ... Winton
oke ... Raeford
yde ... Swan Quarter
edett ... Statesville
ackson ... Sylva
Johnston ... Smithfield
Jones ... Trenton
Lee ... Sanford
Lenoir ... Kinston
Lincoln ... Lincolnton
Macon ... Franklin
Madison ... Marshall
Martin ... Williamston
McDowell ... Marion
Mecklenburg ... Charlotte
Mitchell ... Bakersville
Montgomery ... Troy
Moore ... Carthage
Nash ... Nashville
New Hanover ... Wilmington
Northampton ... Jackson
Onslow ... Jacksonville
Orange ... Hillsborough
Pamlico ... Bayboro
Pasquotank ... Elizabeth City
Pender ... Burgaw
Perquimans ... Hertford
Person ... Roxboro
Pitt ... Greenville
Polk ... Columbus
Randolph ... Asheboro
Richmond ... Lumberton
Rockingham ... Wentworth
Rowan ... Salisbury
Rutherford ... Rutherfordton
Sampson ... Clinton
Scotland ... Laurinburg
Stanly ... Albemarle
Stokes ... Danbury
Surry ... Dobson
Swain ... Bryson City
Transylvania ... Brevard
Tyrrell ... Columbia
Union ... Monroe
Vance ... Henderson
Wake ... Raleigh
Warren ... Warrenton
Washington ... Plymouth
Watauga ... Boone
Wayne ... Goldsboro
Wilkes ... Wilkesboro
Wilson ... Wilson
Yadkin ... Yadkinville
Yancey ... Burnsville

COMPLETE LIST OF

CITIES AND TOWNS

1990 Census
• County Seats

bbottsburg ... 13-B7
berdeen 2,700 ... 13-A6
bner ... 6-C4
bshers ... 6-A2
dvance ... 6-B3,28-C1
dvent Crossroads ... 25-B6
hoskie 4,391 ... 8-A4
lamance 258 ... 7-B6,29-C8
lbermarle • 14,939 ... 6-D4
lbertson ... 14-A2
britton ... 8-D3,14-A3
ert ... 8-B1
exander ... 5-C5
exander Mills 662 ... 5-D7
lexis ... 6-D2,20-B1
llen ... 6-D3,20-C4
llensville ... 7-A7
lliance • 583 ... 9-D5
ltamahaw ... 7-B5
mmon ... 13-A8
nderson ... 7-B6
ndrews • 2,551 ... 4-D2
ngier 2,235 ... 7-C7
nnadale ... 14-B3
nsonville 614 ... 12-A4
ntioch ... 13-A6
pex 4,968 ... 7-C7,27-E5
quadale ... 6-D4
quone ... 4-D3
raphoe • 430 ... 15-A5
rarat ... 6-A3
rcadia ... 28-C2
rchdale 6,913 ... 6-B4,28-D4
rchers Lodge ... 8-C1
rcola ... 8-A2
rden ... 5-C5
rdulusa ... 22-C1
rlington 795 ... 6-B2
rnold ... 28-D2
sh ... 14-C1
sheboro • 16,362 ... 7-C5,29-F6
sheville • 61,607 ... 5-C5,18-A4
shford ... 5-C7
shland ... 5-A7
shland ... 7-A5
shland ... 9-B5
shley Heights ... 13-A6
skewville 201 ... 8-B4
skin ... 8-D4
tkinson 275 ... 14-B2
tlantic ... 15-A6
tlantic Beach 1,938 ... 15-B5
twood ... 28-B1
uburn ... 27-F8
ulander 1,209 ... 8-B4
urelian Springs ... 8-A2
urora 654 ... 9-D5
ustin ... 6-A2
utryville 166 ... 13-A8
venton ... 8-B2
von ... 9-C8
yden 4,740 ... 8-C3
ydlett ... 9-A7
yersville ... 6-A4
achelor ... 15-A5
Badin ... 6-D4
Bahama ... 7-B7,27-A5
Bailey 553 ... 8-C2
Bakers Crossroads ... 7-A5
Bakersville • 332 ... 5-B6
Baldwin ... 5-A8
Balfour ... 24-B4
Balsam ... 4-C4
Balsam Grove ... 4-D4
Bandana ... 5-B6
Banner Elk 933 ... 5-B7
Bannertown ... 6-A3
Barclaysville ... 7-C7
Barco ... 9-A7
Barker Heights ... 24-B4
Barkers Creek ... 22-F3
Barnardsville ... 5-C5
Barnesville ... 13-B7
Barriers Mill ... 6-D3
Bat Cave ... 5-C6
Bath 154 ... 9-C5
Baton ... 5-C8
Battleboro 447 ... 8-B3
Bayboro • 733 ... 9-D5
Bayleaf ... 27-C7
Baynes ... 7-B6
Bayview ... 9-C5
Beamans Cross Roads ... 8-D1
Bear Creek ... 7-C6
Beard ... 22-B2
Bear Grass 77 ... 8-C4
Bearpond ... 7-B8
Beaufort • 3,808 ... 15-B5
Beautancus ... 8-D2
Belcross ... 9-A6
Belew Creek ... 6-B4
Belfast ... 8-C2
Belgrade ... 14-A4
Belhaven 2,269 ... 9-C5
Bells Fork ... 24-C2
Belltown ... 7-B8
Belmont 8,434 ... 6-D2,20-C2
Belvidere ... 9-A5
Belwood 631 ... 5-C8
Bennett ... 7-C5
Benson 2,810 ... 7-D8
Bentonville ... 8-D1
Berea ... 7-A7
Bertha ... 9-A7
Bertie ... 9-B5
Bessemer City 4,698 ... 5-D8
Bethania ... 6-B3,28-A1
Bethany ... 7-A5
Bethel ... 7-A6
Bethel 1,842 ... 8-C3
Bethel ... 9-B6
Bethel Hill ... 7-A7
Bethesda ... 27-C5
Beulah ... 9-C6
Beulaville 933 ... 14-A3
Bilboa ... 27-C5
Biltmore Forest 1,327 ... 18-C4
Birdtown ... 22-F3
Biscoe 1,484 ... 7-D5
Black Creek 615 ... 8-C2
Black Jack ... 8-C4
Black Mountain 5,418 ... 5-C6
Blackwood Station ... 26-C3
Bladenboro 1,821 ... 13-B7
Blaine ... 6-C4
Blands ... 26-D4
Blounts Creek ... 9-D5
Blowing Rock 1,257 ... 5-B7
Bluefield ... 13-B8
Bluff ... 4-C4
Bobbitt ... 7-B8
Bogue ... 14-B4
Boiling Spring Lakes 1,650 ... 14-C2
Boiling Springs 2,445 ... 5-D7
Bolivia 228 ... 14-C2
Bolton 531 ... 14-C1
Bonlee ... 7-C6
Bonnerton ... 9-D5
Bonnie Doon ... 13-A7,22-B1
Bonsal ... 7-C7
Boomer ... 6-B1
Boone • 12,915 ... 5-B7
Boonville 1,009 ... 6-B3
Bostic 371 ... 5-D7
Bottom ... 6-A2
Bowdens ... 14-A2
Bowmore ... 13-A6
Brasstown ... 4-D2
Brevard 5,388 ... 5-D5
Brickhaven ... 7-C7
Bridgeton 453 ... 15-A5,25-D6
Bringham Heights ... 18-B3
Brinkleyville ... 8-B2
Broad Creek ... 15-B5
Broadway 973 ... 7-D7
Brock ... 22-F2
Brookford 451 ... 6-C1,25-B6
Brooks Cross Roads ... 6-B2
Brook Valley ... 24-B2
Browns Crossroads ... 29-F8
Bruce ... 8-C3
Brunswick 302 ... 13-C8
Bryantown ... 8-A3
Bryson City • 1,145 ... 4-C3,22-F3
Buckhorn ... 7-B6,26-B2
Buckhorn Cross Roads ... 8-C2
Buckner ... 5-C5
Buena Vista ... 18-C4
Buie ... 13-B6
Buies Creek ... 7-D7
Buladean ... 5-B6
Bullock ... 7-A8
Bunn 364 ... 8-B1
Bunnlevel ... 7-D7
Burch ... 6-B2
Burgaw • 1,807 ... 14-B2
Burghill ... 13-C8
Burlington 39,498 ... 7-B6,29-B8
Burnsville ... 12-A4
Burnsville • 1,482 ... 5-B6
Burton ... 27-B6
Busick ... 5-C6,29-A6
Butner ... 7-B7,27-A6
Buxton ... 9-D8
Bynum ... 7-C6,26-E3
Cahaba ... 8-B4
Calabash 1,210 ... 14-C1
Calahain ... 6-B3
Caldwell ... 7-B7,26-A4
Calico ... 8-C4
California ... 8-A4
California ... 8-C3
Calvander ... 26-C3
Calypso 481 ... 8-D2
Camden • ... 9-A6
Cameron 215 ... 7-D6
Campbell ... 6-A4
Camp Springs ... 7-B6
Candler ... 5-C5
Candor 748 ... 7-D5
Cannons Crossroads ... 24-C2
Canto ... 5-C5
Canton 3,790 ... 4-C4
Canton ... 9-D5
Capernium ... 28-B1
Carbonton ... 7-C6
Caroleen ... 5-D7
Carolina Beach 3,630 ... 14-C2
Carpenter ... 27-E5
Carrboro 11,553 ... 7-B7,26-D3
Carthage • 976 ... 7-D6
Carvers ... 14-B1
Cary 43,858 ... 7-C7,27-E6
Casar 328 ... 5-C7
Cashiers ... 4-D4
Castaha ... 8-B2
Castle Hayne ... 14-B2
Caswell Beach 175 ... 14-D2
Catawba 467 ... 6-C2
Catherine Lake ... 14-A3
Cedar Creek ... 13-A7
Cedar Falls ... 7-C5,29-F6
Cedar Grove ... 7-B6,26-A2
Cedar Hill ... 6-D4
Cedar Island ... 15-A6
Cedar Lodge ... 28-E3
Cedar Mountain ... 5-D5
Celo ... 5-C6
Centerville 115 ... 8-B2
Cerro Gordo 227 ... 13-C7
Chadbourn 2,005 ... 13-C7
Chalybeate Springs ... 7-C7
Champion ... 6-B1
Chapel Hill 38,719 ... 7-B7,26-C3
Charity ... 14-A2
Charles ... 6-B2
Charlotte • 395,934 ... 6-D2,20-C3
Cheeks Crossroads ... 26-B2
Cheoah ... 4-D2,22-F2
Cherokee ... 4-C3,22-F3
Cherry ... 9-B6
Cherry Grove ... 13-C7
Cherry Lane ... 6-A2
Cherryville 4,756 ... 5-D8
Chimney Rock ... 5-C6
China Grove 2,732 ... 6-C3
Chinquapin ... 14-A3
Chocowinity 624 ... 8-C4
Churchland ... 6-C3,28-E1
Claremont 980 ... 6-C1
Clarkton 739 ... 13-B8
Clayton 4,756 ... 7-C8
Clegg ... 27-D5
Clement ... 13-A8
Clemmons 6,020 ... 6-B3,28-B1
Clemmons Station ... 28-C1
Cliffdale ... 13-A7,22-B1
Cliffside ... 5-D7
Clifton ... 5-A8
Climax ... 7-B5,29-D6
Clinton • 8,204 ... 14-A1
Clyde 1,041 ... 4-C4
Coats 1,493 ... 7-D8
Cofield 407 ... 9-A5
Cognad ... 13-A5
Coinjock ... 9-A7
Colerain 139 ... 9-B5
Coleridge ... 7-C5
Colfax ... 28-B4
Colington ... 9-B7
Collettsville ... 5-B7
Colon ... 7-C6
Columbia • 836 ... 9-B6
Columbus 812 ... 5-D6
Comfort ... 14-A3
Como 71 ... 8-A4
Concord ... 14-A2
Concord • 27,347 ... 6-D3,20-B4
Concord ... 7-A7
Conetoe 292 ... 8-C3
Connaritsa ... 8-B4
Connellys Springs 1,349 ... 5-C8
Conover 5,465 ... 6-C1,25-B6
Conway 759 ... 8-A4
Cooleemee 971 ... 6-C3
Cool Spring ... 6-C2
Corapeake ... 9-A5
Core Point ... 9-C5
Corinth ... 7-C7
Corinth ... 8-B2
Cornatzer ... 6-B3
Cornelius 2,581 ... 6-C2,20-A3
Cornwall ... 7-A8
Corolla ... 9-A7
Costin ... 14-B2
Cotton Grove ... 28-F2
Council ... 14-B1
Courtney ... 6-B3
Cove City 497 ... 8-D4
Covington ... 13-A5
Cox Crossing ... 8-C4
Cozart ... 27-B6
Crabtree ... 4-C4
Craggy ... 18-A3
Cramerton 2,371 ... 6-D2,20-C1
Cranberry ... 5-B7
Creedmoor 1,504 ... 27-B7
Creek Deep ... 12-A4
Creswell 361 ... 9-B6
Crisp ... 8-C3
Croatan ... 15-A5
Crouse ... 5-D8
Crowders ... 6-D1,20-C1
Cruso ... 5-D5
Crutchfield ... 6-B3
Culberson ... 4-D1
Cullasaja ... 4-D3
Cullowhee ... 4-D4
Cumberland ... 22-C1
Currie ... 14-B2
Currituck • ... 9-A7
Dallas 3,012 ... 6-D1,20-B1
Damascus ... 29-D8
Dana ... 5-D6
Danbury • 119 ... 6-A4
Darby ... 5-B8
Darden ... 9-B5
Davidson 4,046 ... 6-C2,20-A3
Davis ... 15-A6
Dawson ... 8-D3
Deep Gap ... 5-B8
Deep River ... 28-B4
Deep Run ... 14-A3
Delco ... 14-C2
Dellwood ... 4-C4,22-E4
Delway ... 14-A2
Democrat ... 5-C5
Denton 1,292 ... 6-C4
Denver ... 6-C2,20-A2
Deppe ... 14-A4
Derby ... 7-D5
Dexter ... 7-A8
Diggs ... 13-A5
Dillsboro 95 ... 4-D3,22-F3
Dixon ... 14-B3
Dobbersville ... 8-D1
Dobbins Heights 1,144 ... 13-A5
Dobson • 1,195 ... 6-A3
Dodgetown ... 6-A4
Dodsons Crossroads ... 26-C3
Dortches 840 ... 30-A3
Dover 451 ... 8-D3
Dozier ... 28-A1
Drewry ... 8-A1
Drexel 1,746 ... 5-C7
Duart ... 13-A7
Dublin 246 ... 13-B7
Duck ... 9-B7
Dudley ... 8-D2
Dudley Shoals ... 5-C8
Duncan ... 7-C7
Dundarrach ... 13-A6
Dunn 8,336 ... 7-D8
Durants Neck ... 9-B6
Durham • 136,611 ... 7-B7
Durham • 136,611 ... 25-E7,26-C4
Eagle Springs ... 7-D5
Earl 230 ... 5-D8
Earley ... 8-B4
East Arcadia 468 ... 14-B1
East Bend 619 ... 6-B3
East Flat Rock ... 5-D5,24-C4
East Lake ... 9-B7
East Laurinburg 302 ... 13-B6
East Lumberton ... 13-B7
Eastover ... 22-B2
Eastwood ... 7-D6
Eden 15,238 ... 7-A5
Edenton • 5,268 ... 9-B5
Edgecombe ... 14-B3
Edgemont ... 5-B7
Edneyville ... 5-D6
Edward ... 9-D5
Efland ... 7-B6,26-B2
Ela ... 4-C3,22-F3
Elams ... 8-A2
Elberon ... 8-A1
Eldorado ... 6-C4
Eli Whitney ... 7-B6,26-D1
Elizabeth City • 14,292 ... 9-A6
Elizabethtown • 3,704 ... 13-B8
Elkin 3,790 ... 6-B2
Elk Park 486 ... 5-B7
Ellenboro 514 ... 5-D7
Eller ... 6-B4,28-C2
Ellerbe 1,132 ... 13-A5
Ellijay ... 4-D3
Elliott ... 14-A2
Elm City 1,624 ... 8-C2
Elm Grove ... 8-D3
Elmwood ... 6-C2
Elon College 4,394 ... 7-B5,29-B8
Ely ... 22-A2
Embro ... 8-A2
Emerald Isle 2,434 ... 15-B5
Emerson ... 13-B8
Emery ... 7-D5
Emit ... 8-C1
Emma ... 18-B3
Enfield 3,082 ... 8-B3
Engelhard ... 9-C7
Enka ... 5-C5
Enon ... 6-B3
Enterprise ... 28-C2
Epsom ... 7-B8
Ernul ... 8-D4
Erwin 4,061 ... 7-D7
Essex ... 8-B2
Ether ... 7-D5
Etowah ... 5-D5,24-B3
Eubanks ... 26-C3
Eureka 282 ... 8-C2
Everetts 143 ... 8-C4
Evergreen ... 13-B7
Exum ... 14-C1
Fair Bluff 1,068 ... 13-C7
Fairbrook ... 25-B6
Fairfield ... 9-C6
Fair Grove ... 28-D3
Fairmont 2,489 ... 13-B6
Fairplains ... 6-B1
Fairport ... 7-B8
Fairview ... 26-B3
Fairview ... 6-D3,20-D4
Fairview Cross Roads ... 6-A3
Faison 701 ... 8-D2
Falcon 216 ... 7-D8
Falkland 108 ... 8-C3
Falling Creek ... 8-D3
Falls ... 27-C7
Falls Gilreath ... 6-B2
Fallston 498 ... 5-D8
Farmer ... 6-C4
Farmington ... 6-B3
Farmville • 4,392 ... 8-C3
Fayetteville • 75,695 ... 13-A7,22-B1
Fearrington ... 7-C7,26-E4
Ferguson ... 5-B8
Fisherville ... 28-B2
Flat Rock ... 5-D5,24-C4
Fletcher 2,787 ... 5-D5,24-A3
Flint Hill ... 6-C4,29-E5
Florence ... 9-D5
Folkstone ... 14-B3
Fontana Village ... 4-C2,22-F1
Forest ... 25-D5
Forest City 7,475 ... 5-D7
Fork ... 6-C3
Fort Barnwell ... 8-D4
Fort Bragg ... 13-A7
Fort Fisher ... 14-C2
Fort Landing ... 9-B7
Fountain ... 14-A3
Fountain 445 ... 8-C3
Fountain Fork ... 8-B3
Fountain Hill ... 12-A4
Four Oaks 1,308 ... 7-D8
Francisco ... 6-A3
Franklin 2,873 ... 4-D3
Franklin ... 6-C3
Franklinton 1,615 ... 7-B8,27-B8
Franklinville 666 ... 7-C5,29-F7
Freeland ... 14-C1
Freeman ... 14-C1
Freezor ... 28-F2
Fremont 1,710 ... 8-C2
Friendship ... 6-B4,28-B4
Friendship ... 7-C7,27-B5
Frisco ... 9-D8
Frog Level ... 24-C1
Fruitland ... 5-D6
Frying Pan Landing ... 9-B7
Fuquay-Varina 4,562 ... 7-C7
Galatia ... 8-A4
Gamewell 3,357 ... 5-C7
Gap ... 6-A3
Gardners Store ... 7-D5
Garland 746 ... 14-B1
Garner 14,967 ... 7-C8,27-F7
Garysburg 1,057 ... 8-A3
Gaston 1,003 ... 8-A3
Gastonia 54,732 ... 6-D1,20-C1
Gates ... 9-A5
Gatesville • 308 ... 9-A5
Gaylord ... 9-C5
Genlee ... 27-D5
Germantown ... 6-B4
Ghio ... 13-A5
Gibson 532 ... 14-B5
Gibsonville 3,441 ... 7-B5,29-B8
Glen Alpine 563 ... 5-C7
Glendon ... 7-C6
Glenola ... 6-C4,29-D5
Glen Raven ... 7-B6,29-B8
Glenview ... 8-B2
Glenville ... 4-D4
Gliden ... 9-A5
Globe ... 5-B7
Gneiss ... 4-D3
Godwin 77 ... 7-D7
Gold Hill ... 6-C3
Goldsboro • 40,709 ... 8-D2
Goldston 299 ... 7-C6
Gordonton ... 7-B6,28-E3
Gorman ... 7-B7,27-B6
Goshen ... 8-D1
Grace Chapel ... 25-A5
Graham • 10,426 ... 7-B6,26-B1
Grainger ... 8-D3
Grandview ... 4-D1
Grandy ... 9-A7
Granite Falls 3,253 ... 5-C8,25-A5
Granite Quarry 1,646 ... 6-C3
Grantham ... 8-D2,25-E6
Grantsboro ... 9-D5
Grays Chapel ... 7-C5,29-E7
Green Level ... 27-E5
Greensboro • 183,521 ... 7-B5,29-B5
Greenville • 44,972 ... 8-C3,24-B1
Griffins Crossroads ... 26-F3
Grifton 2,393 ... 8-D3
Grimesland 469 ... 8-C4
Grissom ... 7-B8,27-B7
Grover 516 ... 5-D8
Guide ... 13-C7
Gulbreth ... 7-B7
Gulf ... 7-C6
Gull Rock ... 9-C7
Gum Lake ... 9-C6
Gum Neck Landing ... 9-C7
Gumtree ... 28-C2
Guthrie ... 28-B3
Guyton ... 13-B7
Halifax • 327 ... 8-A3
Hallsboro ... 13-C8
Halls Mills ... 6-B1
Hamer ... 7-A6
Hamilton 544 ... 8-B4
Hamlet 6,196 ... 13-A5
Hampstead ... 14-B3
Hamptonville ... 6-B2
Handellman ... 26-E1
Harbinger ... 9-B7
Hargetts Store ... 14-A3
Harkers Island ... 15-B6
Harlowe ... 15-A5
Harmony 431 ... 6-B2
Harrells 187 ... 14-B2
Harrellsville 106 ... 9-A5
Harris ... 5-D7
Harrisburg 1,625 ... 6-D3,20-B4
Hartsease ... 8-B3
Hassell 95 ... 8-B4
Hasty ... 13-B6
Hatteras ... 9-D8
Havelock 20,268 ... 15-A5
Haw River 1,855 ... 7-B6,26-B1
Hayesville 279 ... 4-D2
Hayne ... 13-A8
Haywood ... 7-C7
Hazelwood 1,678 ... 4-C4
Healing Springs ... 6-C4
Heathsville ... 8-B2
Heaton ... 5-B7
Helton ... 5-A8
Hemlock ... 5-A7
Henderson • 15,655 ... 8-A1
Hendersonville 7,284 ... 5-D5,24-B3
Henrico ... 8-A2
Henrietta ... 5-D7
Henry River ... 5-C8,25-B5
Hertford • 2,105 ... 9-B6
Hester ... 7-B7,27-A7
Hickory 28,301 ... 6-C1,25-B6
Hickory North ... 25-A6
Hiddenite ... 6-B2
Highfalls ... 7-C5
Highlands 948 ... 4-D4
High Point 69,496 ... 6-B4,28-C4
High Rock ... 6-C4
High Shoals 605 ... 6-D1,20-B1
Hightowers ... 7-A6
Hildebran 790 ... 5-C8,25-B5
Hillsborough • 4,263 ... 7-B7,26-B3
Hillsville ... 29-E5
Hobbton ... 8-D1
Hobgood 435 ... 8-B3
Hobucken ... 9-D6
Hoffman 348 ... 13-A5
Hoke ... 9-C5
Holden Beach 626 ... 14-C1
Hollis ... 5-D7
Hollister ... 8-B2
Holly Grove ... 9-A5,28-E2
Holly Ridge 728 ... 14-B3
Holly Springs 908 ... 7-C7
Hollyville ... 9-D5
Hood Swamp ... 8-D2
Hookerton 422 ... 8-C3
Hoopers Creek ... 24-A4
Hope Mills 8,184 ... 13-A7,22-C1
Horse Shoe ... 5-D5
Hot Springs 478 ... 4-B4
House ... 8-C4,24-A1
Hubert ... 14-B4
Hudson 2,819 ... 5-C8
Huntersville 3,014 ... 6-D2,20-B3
Huntsville ... 6-B3
Hurdle Mills ... 7-B7
Hydro ... 6-D4
Indian Trail 1,942 ... 12-A3,20-D4
Inez ... 8-B2
Ingalls ... 5-B7
Ingleside ... 8-B1
Ingold ... 14-A1
Ironhill ... 13-C7
Iron Station ... 6-D1,20-A1
Ivanhoe ... 14-B1
Jackson • 592 ... 8-A3
Jackson Creek ... 28-F3
Jackson Hamlet ... 7-D6
Jackson Hill ... 6-C4
Jackson Springs ... 7-D5
Jacksonville • 30,013 ... 14-B3
James City ... 14-A4,25-E6
Jamestown 2,600 ... 6-B4,29-C5
Jamesville 612 ... 9-C5
Janeiro ... 15-A5
Jarvisburg ... 9-B7
Jason ... 8-D3
Jasper ... 8-D4
Jefferson • 1,300 ... 5-A8
Jericho ... 7-B6
Jessama ... 9-C5
Johns ... 13-B6
Johnsonville ... 7-D6
Jonas Ridge ... 5-B7
Jonathan ... 22-E4
Jonesville 1,549 ... 6-B2
Joyners Crossroads ... 30-B3
Jugtown ... 7-C5
Julian ... 7-B5,29-D7
Justice ... 8-B2
Kannapolis 29,696 ... 6-C3,20-A4
Katesville ... 7-B8
Kearney ... 8-B1
Keener ... 14-A1
Kelford 204 ... 8-B4
Kellum ... 14-A4
Kelly ... 14-B1
Kenansville • 856 ... 14-A2
Kenly 1,549 ... 8-C2
Kennebec ... 7-C7
Kennedy ... 26-A3
Kernersville 10,836 ... 6-B4,28-A4
Kerr ... 30-D3
Kilkenny ... 9-C6
Kill Devil Hills 4,238 ... 9-B8
Kimesville ... 7-B5,29-C8
King 4,059 ... 6-B3
Kings Creek ... 5-B8
Kings Mountain 8,763 ... 5-D8
Kinston • 25,295 ... 8-D3
Kipling ... 7-C7
Kittrell 228 ... 7-B8
Kitty Hawk 1,937 ... 9-B7
Knap of Reeds ... 27-A6
Knightdale 1,884 ... 7-C8,27-E8
Knotts Island ... 9-A7
Kornegay ... 14-A2
Kuhns ... 14-A4
Kure Beach 619 ... 14-C2
Lacey ... 28-D2
La Grange 2,805 ... 8-D3
Lake Junaluska ... 4-C4
Lake Landing ... 9-C7
Lake Lure 691 ... 5-D6
Lake Toxaway ... 4-D4
Lakeview ... 7-D6
Lake Waccamaw 954 ... 14-C1
Lambert ... 6-D3
Lambeth's ... 28-E3
Lamm ... 8-C2
Landis 2,333 ... 6-C3,20-A4
Langley Crossroads ... 30-B3
Lansing 171 ... 5-A8
Latham ... 8-C4
Lattimore 183 ... 5-D7
Lauada ... 4-D3
Laurel Hill ... 13-A5
Laurel Park 1,322 ... 24-B3
Laurel Springs ... 6-A1
Laurinburg • 11,643 ... 13-B6
Lawrence ... 8-B3
Lawsonville ... 6-A4
Lawsonville ... 7-A5
Laxon ... 5-B8
Leasburg ... 7-A6
Leggett 108 ... 8-B3
Leicester ... 5-C5
Leland 1,801 ... 14-C2
Lemon Springs ... 7-D6
Lena ... 13-A7
Lenoir • 14,192 ... 5-B8
Level Cross ... 29-D6
Levelcross ... 6-A3
Lewis ... 7-A8
Lewiston Woodville 788 ... 8-B4
Lewisville ... 28-B1
Lexington • 16,581 ... 6-C4,28-E2
Liberia ... 8-A2
Liberty 2,047 ... 7-C5,29-D7
Liddell ... 8-D2
Lilesville 468 ... 12-A4
Lillington • 2,048 ... 7-D7
Lima ... 8-D4
Lincolnton • 6,847 ... 6-C1,20-A1
Lindell ... 8-C2
Linden 180 ... 7-D7
Lineberry ... 29-D7
Linville ... 5-B7
Linville Falls ... 5-B7
Linwood ... 28-F1
Lisbon ... 13-B8
Little River ... 5-D5
Little Switzerland ... 5-C6
Littleton 691 ... 8-A2
Lizzie ... 8-C3
Lobelia ... 7-D6
Locust 1,940 ... 6-D3
Locust Hill ... 7-A6
Logan ... 5-D7
Lola ... 15-A6
Long Beach 3,816 ... 14-D2
Long Creek ... 14-B2
Longhurst ... 7-A7
Long Island ... 6-C2
Long View 3,229 ... 5-C8,25-B5
Longwood ... 14-C1
Loray ... 6-C2
Louisburg 3,037 ... 8-B1
Lowell 2,704 ... 6-D2,20-C1
Lowesville ... 6-D2,20-B2
Low Gap ... 6-A2
Lowland ... 9-D6
Lucama 933 ... 8-C2
Lucia ... 6-D2,20-B2
Lumber Bridge 109 ... 13-A7
Lumberton 18,601 ... 13-B7
Luther ... 5-C5
Lynn ... 5-D6
Lyons ... 27-A6
Macclesfield ... 8-C3
Macedonia ... 27-F6
Macks ... 7-D8
Macon 154 ... 8-A2
Madison 2,371 ... 6-A4
Maggie Valley 185 ... 4-C4,22-E4
Magnolia 747 ... 14-A2
Maiden 2,574 ... 6-C1
Makatoka ... 14-C1
Mamers ... 7-D7
Manchester ... 13-A7
Mandale ... 26-D2
Mangum ... 12-A4
Manly ... 7-D6
Manns Harbor ... 9-B7
Mansfield ... 15-B5
Manson ... 8-A1
Manteo • 991 ... 9-B8
Maple Hill ... 14-B3
Maple Springs ... 5-B8
Mapleton ... 8-A4
Mapleville ... 8-B1
Marble ... 4-D2
Margarettsville ... 8-A3
Maribel ... 9-D5
Marion • 4,765 ... 5-C6
Marshall • 809 ... 5-C5
Marshallberg ... 15-B6
Mars Hill 1,611 ... 5-C5
Marshville 2,020 ... 12-A3
Marston ... 13-A5
Masonboro ... 30-F4
Mathis ... 28-B3
Matthews 13,651 ... 12-A2,20-B3
Maury ... 8-C3
Maxton 2,373 ... 13-B6
Mayodan 2,471 ... 6-A4
Maysville 892 ... 14-A4
McAdenville 830 ... 20-C1
McConnell ... 7-D5
McCray ... 26-A1
McCullers ... 7-C7
McDade ... 26-A2
McDonald 88 ... 13-B6
McFarlan 98 ... 12-A4
McGrady ... 6-A1
McLeansville ... 29-B7
Meadows ... 6-A4
Mebane 4,754 ... 7-B6,26-B1
Meege Cross Roads ... 9-B5
Melanchron ... 29-E7
Menlo ... 8-A4
Merriman ... 15-A5
Merritt ... 9-D5
Merry Hill ... 9-B5
Merry Oaks ... 7-C7
Mesic 310 ... 9-D5
Micaville ... 5-B6
Michfield ... 7-C5
Micro 417 ... 8-C1
Middlesex 730 ... 8-C1
Middletown ... 9-C7
Midland ... 6-D3,20-C4
Midway ... 14-A1
Midway ... 7-B5
Milburnie ... 7-C8,27-E8
Mildred ... 8-B3
Miles ... 26-B2
Millboro ... 29-E6
Millbrook ... 27-D7
Millers Creek ... 6-B1
Millersville ... 6-C1
Millingport ... 6-D4
Mill Spring ... 5-D6
Mills River ... 5-D5,24-A3
Milton 185 ... 7-A6
Milwaukee ... 8-A4
Mineral Springs ... 12-A3,20-E4
Minneapolis ... 5-B7
Minnesott Beach 266 ... 15-A5
Mint Hill 11,567 ... 6-D3,20-D4
Mintonsville ... 9-A5
Mocksville • 3,399 ... 6-B3
Momeyer ... 8-B2
Moncure ... 7-C7
Monroe • 16,127 ... 12-A3,20-E4
Monroeton ... 7-B5
Montreat 693 ... 5-C6
Montrose ... 13-A6
Moores Springs ... 6-A4
Mooresville 9,317 ... 6-C2
Moravian ... 6-B1
Morehead City 6,046 ... 15-B5
Morgans Corner ... 9-A6
Morganton • 15,085 ... 5-C7
Moriah ... 7-B7
Morrisville 1,022 ... 7-C7,27-E5
Morven 590 ... 12-A4
Mountain Home ... 5-D5,24-B4
Mountain View ... 6-D1
Mount Airy 7,156 ... 6-A3
Mount Energy ... 27-A7
Mount Gilead 1,336 ... 6-D4
Mount Gould ... 9-B5
Mount Holly 7,710 ... 6-D2,20-C2
Mount Olive ... 6-A3
Mount Olive 4,582 ... 8-D2
Mount Pleasant 1,027 ... 6-D3
Mount Sterling ... 4-C4,22-D4
Mount Ulla ... 6-C2
Mount Vernon Springs ... 7-C6
Mount Zion ... 5-B8
Moyock ... 9-A6
Muddy Creek ... 28-C1
Murfreesboro 2,580 ... 8-A4
Murphy 1,575 ... 4-D1
Murphytown ... 14-B1
Nags Head 1,838 ... 9-B8
Nakina ... 13-C8
Nantahala ... 4-D2
Nashville • 3,617 ... 8-B2
Nathans Creek ... 6-A1
Nebo ... 5-C7
Nelson ... 7-C7,25-F8
Neuse ... 7-B8,27-D7
New Bern • 17,363 ... 14-A4,25-E5
New Bridge ... 18-A3
Newfoundland ... 9-B6
New Hill ... 7-C7
New Holland ... 9-C6
New Hope ... 8-B1,27-E8
New Hope ... 8-C2
Newland • 645 ... 5-B7
New London 414 ... 6-D4
New Market ... 29-E5
Newport 2,516 ... 15-A5
New Salem ... 6-D3,29-E6
Newton • 9,304 ... 6-C1
Newton Grove 511 ... 8-D1
Newtons Cross Road ... 14-B2
New Topsail Beach ... 14-B3
Nixonton ... 9-B6
Norlina 996 ... 8-A1
Norman 105 ... 7-D5
North Adams ... 6-B2
North Belmont ... 6-D2,20-C2
North Cove ... 5-C7
North Harlowe ... 15-A5
North Side ... 27-B6
Northside ... 7-B7
North Wilkesboro 3,384 ... 6-B1
Norton ... 4-D4
Norwood 1,617 ... 6-D4
Nye ... 27-A8
Oakboro 600 ... 6-D3
Oak City 389 ... 8-B4
Oak Grove ... 27-C5
Oak Hill ... 7-A7
Oakland ... 4-D4
Oak Park ... 4-D1
Oak Ridge ... 6-B4,28-A4
Oaks ... 26-C2
Obids ... 5-B8
Ocean Isle Beach 523 ... 14-C1
O. & C. Junction ... 27-C5
Ocracoke ... 15-A7
Oine ... 8-A1
Old Dock ... 13-C8
Old Ford ... 8-C4
Old Fort 720 ... 5-C6
Oldtown ... 28-A1
Old Trap ... 9-A7
Oliver Cross Roads ... 14-A4
Olivia ... 7-D6
Olympia ... 9-D5
Olyphic ... 13-C8
Onvil ... 7-D5
Ophir ... 6-C4
Orange Grove ... 7-B6,26-C2
Ore Knob ... 6-A1
Oriental 786 ... 15-A5
Orrum 103 ... 13-B7
Osceola ... 7-B5
Ossipee ... 7-B5,29-A8
Oteen ... 18-B4
Otway ... 15-A6
Oxford • 7,913 ... 7-A8
Pactolus ... 8-C4
Paint Gap ... 5-B6
Palmyra ... 8-B4
Pamlico ... 15-A5
Pamlico Beach ... 9-C5
Pantego 171 ... 9-C5
Panther Creek ... 22-E4
Parks Crossroads ... 29-F7
Parkton 367 ... 13-A7
Parkwood ... 7-D6,27-D5
Parmele 321 ... 8-C4
Patterson ... 5-B8
Patterson Springs 690 ... 5-D8
Peachtree ... 4-D2
Pearces ... 8-B1
Pea Ridge ... 5-D6
Pee Dee ... 13-A5
Pee Dee ... 6-D4
Pekin ... 13-A5
Pekin ... 7-D5
Pelham ... 7-A6
Pembroke 2,241 ... 13-B6
Penderlea ... 14-B2
Penelope ... 25-B5
Penland ... 5-B6
Penrose ... 5-D5
Pensacola ... 5-C6
Perfection ... 8-D4
Petersburg ... 14-A3
Pfafftown ... 28-A1
Philadelphus ... 13-B6
Pikeville 598 ... 8-C2
Pilot ... 8-B1
Pinebluff 876 ... 13-A6
Pine Grove ... 15-A5
Pine Hall ... 6-A4
Pinehurst 5,103 ... 7-D6
Pine Level 1,217 ... 8-C1
Pineola ... 5-B7
Pine Ridge ... 6-A3
Pinetops 1,514 ... 8-C3
Pine Valley ... 25-D6
Pineview ... 7-D6
Pineville 2,970 ... 12-A2,20-D2
Piney Creek ... 6-A1
Piney Green ... 14-B4
Piney Wood ... 14-B2
Pink Hill 547 ... 14-A3
Pinnacle ... 6-A3
Pireway ... 13-C8
Pisgah ... 7-C5
Pittmans Store ... 8-B2
Pittsboro • 1,436 ... 7-C6,26-F3
Plateau ... 5-C8
Pleasant Garden ... 29-C6
Pleasant Gardens ... 5-C6
Pleasant Grove ... 26-A1
Pleasant Grove ... 9-B5
Pleasant Hill ... 14-A3
Pleasant Hill ... 8-A3
Pleasant Ridge ... 29-F7
Plot Mountain ... 6-A3
Plumtree ... 5-B7
Plyler ... 6-D4
Plymouth • 4,328 ... 9-B5
Pocomoke ... 27-B8
Point Harbor ... 9-B7
Polkton 662 ... 12-A4
Polkville 1,514 ... 5-D7
Pollocksville 299 ... 14-A4
Poplar Branch ... 9-A7
Porter ... 6-D4
Portsmouth ... 15-A7
Potecasi ... 8-A4
Potters Hill ... 14-A3
Powells Point ... 9-B7
Powellsville 103 ... 9-B5
Prestonville ... 6-A4
Price ... 6-A4
Princeton 1,181 ... 8-C2
Princeville 1,652 ... 8-B3

Place ..... Population ..... Page Grid
Aberdeen ..... 2,700 ..... 13-A6

Propst Cross Roads.....5-C8
Propst Store.....25-A6
Prospect Hill.....7-B6
Providence.....7-B7
Pumpkin Center..6-C1,20-A1
Purlear.....6-B1
Purnell.....27-C8
Purvis.....13-B6
Quitsna.....8-B4
Raeford • 3,469.....13-A6
Raemon.....13-B6
Rainbow Springs.....4-D3
Raleigh •
207,951.....7-C8,27-E7
Ramseur 1,186...7-C5,29-F7
Ramsey.....5-C8
Ramseytown.....5-B6
Randleman
2,612.....7-C5,29-E6
Ranger.....4-D1
Ranlo 1,650.....20-B1
Ransomville.....9-C5
Raynham 106.....13-B6
Reachland.....12-A4
Redcross.....29-D7
Red Cross.....6-D3
Red Hill.....14-A2
Red Hill.....5-B6
Red Oak 280.....8-B2
Red Springs 3,799.....13-A6
Redwood.....27-B6
Reeds Crossroads.....28-E1
Reedy Creek.....28-D1
Reelsboro.....9-D5
Reidsville 12,183.....7-A5
Ren.....9-C5
Rennert 217.....13-A7
Rhodhiss 638....5-C8,25-A5
Richardson.....13-B7
Richfield 535.....6-D4
Richlands 996.....14-A3
Rich Square 1,058.....8-A4
Riddle.....9-A7
Ridgecrest.....5-C6
Ridgeville.....7-B6
Riegelwood.....14-C2
Riley.....8-B1
River
Bend 2,408...14-A4,25-F5
River Neck.....9-B6
Roanoke
Rapids 15,722.....8-A3
Roaring River.....6-B2
Robbins 970.....7-D5
Robbinsville •
709.....4-D2,22-F1
Roberdel.....13-A5
Robersonville 1,940.....8-C4
Rock Creek.....29-D8
Rockfish.....13-A7
Rockingham • 9,399..13-A5
Rock Spring.....24-B1
Rockwell 1,598.....6-C3
Rocky Mount •
48,997.....8-B2,30-B3
Rocky Point.....14-B2
Rodanthe.....9-C8
Roduco.....9-A5
Rogers Store.....27-C6
Rolesville 572...7-B8,27-D8
Ronda 367.....6-B2
Roper 669.....9-B5
Roseboro 1,441.....14-A1
Rose Hill 1,287.....14-A2
Rose Hill.....18-C4
Roseville.....7-A7
Rosewood.....8-D2
Rosin.....7-D8
Rosman 385.....4-D4
Rougemont.....7-B7
Rowan Mills.....6-C3
Rowland 1,139.....13-B6
Roxboro • 7,332.....7-A7
Roxobel 244.....8-B4
Royal.....9-D5
Ruffin.....7-A5
Rural Hall 1,652.....6-B4
Ruskin.....14-B8
Ruth 366.....5-D7
Rutherfordton • 3,617..5-D7
Rymers Ferry.....22-F1
St. John.....8-A4
St. Johns.....8-D4
St. Johns.....9-B6
St. Pauls 1,992.....13-A7
St. Stephens.....25-B6
Salem.....8-B2
Salemburg 409.....14-A1
Salisbury • 23,087.....6-C3
Salter Path.....15-B5
Saluda 488.....5-D6
Salvo.....9-C8
Samarcand.....7-D5
Samaria.....8-C2
Sand Hill.....18-C3
Sandy Bottom.....8-D3
Sandy Plains.....5-D6
Sandy Ridge.....6-A4
Sanford • 14,475.....7-C6
Santeetlah 47.....22-F1
Saratoga 342.....8-C3
Sarecta.....14-A2
Saxapahaw.....7-B6,26-C1
Scaly.....4-D3
Schley.....7-B7,26-A3
Scotland Neck 2,575....8-B3
Scranton.....9-C6
Scuffleton.....8-C3
Scuppernong.....9-B6
Seaboard 791.....8-A3
Seagrove 244.....7-C5
Sedalia.....29-B7
Sedgefield.....29-C5
Selma 4,600.....8-C1
Semora.....7-A6
Seven Paths.....8-B1
Seven Springs 163.....8-D2
Severn 260.....8-A4
Shallotte 965.....14-C1
Sharpsburg
1,536.....8-B2,30-B3
Shatley Springs.....5-A8
Shawboro.....9-A7
Shaw.....22-B1
Shelby 14,669.....5-D8
Shelmerdine.....8-C4
Shephards.....6-C2
Shiloh.....9-A7
Shooting Creek.....4-D2
Shulls Mills.....5-B7
Sidney.....13-C7
Sidney.....9-C5
Siler City 4,808...7-C6,29-F8
Silk Hope.....26-E1
Siloam.....6-B3
Silverdale.....14-A4
Silver Hill.....28-F2
Silver Valley.....6-C4,28,-F3
Simpson 410.....8-C4
Sioux.....5-B6
Sixforks.....27-D7
Skibo.....22-B1
Skinnersville.....9-B6
Skyland.....5-C5
Sladesville.....9-C6
Sligo.....9-A7
Small.....9-D5
Smithfield • 7,540.....8-C1
Smiths.....13-B7
Smiths Grove.....6-B3
Smithtown.....6-B3
Smyrna.....15-A6
Snow Cap.....7-B6
Snow Hill • 1,378.....8-C3
Sophia.....7-C5,29-E5
South Creek.....9-D5
Southern Pines 9,129...7-D6
South Mills.....9-A6
Southmont.....6-C4
South of the Border.....13-B6
Southport • 2,369.....14-D2
South River.....15-A6
South Salisbury.....6-C3
Sparta • 1,957.....6-A2
Speed 88.....8-B3
Spencer 3,219.....6-C3
Spencer
Mountain 135.....20-B1
Spindale 4,040.....5-D7
Spout Springs.....7-D7
Spring Hill.....8-B3
Spring Hope 1,221.....8-B2
Spring
Lake 7,524...13-A7,22-A1
Spring Creek.....4-C4
Spruce Pine 2,010.....5-B6
Stacy.....15-A6
Staley 204.....7-C5,29-E8
Stallings 2,132.....20-D3
Stallings Cross Roads...8-B2
Stanbury.....14-C1
Stanfield 517.....6-D3
Stanhope.....8-B2
Stanley 2,823.....6-D2,20-B1
Stanleyville.....6-B4
Stantonsburg 782.....8-C2
Star 775.....7-D5
Startown.....25-C6
State Road.....6-A2
Statesville • 17,567.....6-C2
Stecoah.....4-D2,22-F2
Stedman 577.....13-A7
Stem 249.....7-B7
Stocksville.....5-C5
Stokes.....8-C4
Stokesdale 2,134.....6-B4
Stoneville 1,109.....7-A5
Stony Point.....6-C2
Stovall 409.....7-A8
Strabane.....8-D3
Straits.....15-B6
Stratford.....6-A1
Stumpy Point.....9-C7
Sturdivants.....12-A3
Sugar Hill.....5-C6
Suit.....4-D1
Sulpher Springs.....6-A3
Summerfield.....7-B5
Summerlins
Crossroads.....14-A2
Sunburst.....4-D4
Sunbury.....9-A5
Sunset Harbor.....14-C2
Sunshine.....5-D7
Supply.....14-C1
Surf City 970.....14-B3
Surl.....7-A7
Sutphin.....26-D1
Swancreek.....6-B2
Swann.....7-D6
Swannanoa.....5-C6
Swan Quarter •.....9-C6
Swansboro 1,165.....14-B4
Swepsonville.....7-B6,26-C1
Swiss.....5-B5
Sylva • 1,809.....4-D3,22-F4
Tabor City 2,330.....13-C7
Tapoco.....4-C2,22-F1
Tarboro • 11,037.....8-B3
Tar Heel 115.....13-B7
Taylors Bridge.....14-A1
Taylors Store.....8-B2
Taylorsville • 1,566.....6-B1
Teachey 244.....14-B2
Terrell.....6-C2
Terrells.....26-E2
Thermal City.....5-C7
Thomasville
15,915.....6-C4,28-D3
Thurmond.....6-A2
Tillery.....8-B3
Timberlake.....7-B7
Timberland.....13-A6
Tin City.....14-B2
Toast.....6-A3
Tobaccoville.....6-B3
Todd.....5-A8
Tolarsville.....13-B7
Toluca.....5-C8
Tomahawk.....14-B1
Topnot.....7-A6
Topton.....4-D2
Town Creek.....8-C2
Townsville.....8-A1
Trading Ford.....28-F1
Tramway.....7-D6
Trap.....9-B5
Traphill.....6-A2
Trenton • 248.....14-A4
Trent Woods 2,366.....25-E5
Triangle.....6-C2,20-A2
Trinity.....6-B4,28-D4
Triple Springs.....7-A7
Triplett.....5-B8
Trotville.....9-A5
Troutman 1,493.....6-C2
Troy • 3,404.....7-D5
Trust.....4-C4
Tuckasegee.....4-D4
Turkey 234.....14-A2
Turnersburg.....6-B2
Tuscarora.....8-D4
Tuskeegee.....4-C2
Tusquitee.....4-D2
Tuxedo.....5-D5
Twin Oaks.....6-A1
Tyro.....28-E1
Tyron.....5-D6
Ulah.....7-C5
Unaka.....4-D1
Union.....8-A4
Union Cross.....28-B3
Union Grove.....6-B2
Union Ridge.....7-B6
Unionville.....12-A3
University.....26-B3
Uwharrie.....6-D4
Vahalla.....9-B5
Valdese 3,914.....5-C7
Vale.....5-C8
Valle Crucis.....5-B7
Valley Hill.....24-B4
Valmead.....5-B8
Vanceboro 946.....8-D4
Vandalia.....29-C6
Vandemere 299.....9-D5
Vander.....13-A7,22-B2
Vass 670.....7-D6
Vaughan.....8-A2
Verona.....14-B3
Vicksboro.....8-A1
Vienna.....28-A1
Villas.....5-B7
Vultare.....8-A2
Waco 320.....5-D8
Wade 238.....13-A7
Wadesboro • 3,645.....12-A4
Wadeville.....6-D4
Wagoner.....6-B2
Wagram 480.....13-A6
Wake Crossroads.....27-D8
Wakefield.....8-C1
Wake
Forest 5,769...7-B8,27-C8
Walkertown
1,200.....6-B4,28-A3
Wallace 2,939.....14-B2
Wallburg.....6-B4,28-C3
Walnut.....5-C5
Walnut Cove 1,088.....6-B4
Walnut Creek 623.....5-C5
Walstonburg 188.....8-C3
Wanchese.....9-B8
Wards.....13-C7
Warne.....4-D2
Warrensville.....5-A8
Warrenton • 949.....8-A2
Warsaw 2,859.....14-A2
Washington 9,075.....8-C4
Washington Forks.....25-D5
Waterlily.....9-A7
Waterville.....22-D4
Waxhaw
1,294.....12-A2,20-E3
Waynesville •
6,758.....4-C4,22-E4
Wayside.....13-A6
Weaver.....27-B5
Weaverville 2,107.....5-C5
Weddington 3,803.....20-E3
Weeksville.....9-B6
Welcome.....6-B4,28-D2
Weldon 1,392.....8-A3
Wendell 2,822.....8-C1
Wenona.....9-C5
Wentworth •.....7-A5
Wesley Chapel..12-A3,20-E4
Wesser.....4-D3
West Cross Roads.....7-D8
West End.....7-D5
Westfield.....6-A3
West Jefferson 1,002....5-B4
West Mount.....30-B3
West Philadelphia.....7-D5
Westry.....30-A3
Whispering
Pines 1,243.....7-D6
Whitakers 860.....8-B3
White Cross.....26-D2
Whitehead.....6-A1
Whitehurst.....8-C4
White Lake 390.....14-B1
White Oak.....13-B7
White Plains.....6-A3
Whiterock.....5-B5
Whites Chapel.....29-E7
Whiteville • 5,078.....13-C8
Whitsett.....7-B5,29-B8
Whittier.....22-F3
Whortonsville.....9-D5
Whynot.....7-C5
Wilbanks.....8-C3
Wilbar.....6-B1
Wilders Grove.....27-E8
Wilgrove.....6-D3,20-C4
Wilkesboro • 2,573.....6-B1
Willard.....14-B2
Willardville.....27-A5
Williamsboro.....7-A8
Williamsburg.....7-B5
Williamston • 5,503.....8-B4
Wilmar.....8-B4
Wilmington •
55,530.....14-C2,30-D3
Wilson • 36,930.....8-C2
Wilsons Mills.....8-C1
Wilsonville.....7-C7,26-F4
Wilton.....7-B8,27-A7
Windsor • 2,056.....8-B4
Winfall 501.....9-B6
Wingate 2,821.....12-A3
Winslow.....24-B2
Winston-Salem •
143,485.....6-B4,28-B1
Winterville 2,816.....8-C3
Winton • 796.....9-A5
Wise.....8-A1
Wise Fork.....8-D3
Wolf Creek.....4-D1
Wood.....8-B2
Woodard.....8-B4
Woodfin 2,736.....18-A3
Woodington.....8-D3
Woodland 760.....8-A4
Woodlawn.....5-C6
Woodleaf.....6-C3
Woodley.....9-B6
Woodrow.....25-D5
Woodsdale.....7-A7
Woodville.....9-B6
Wrightsville
Beach 2,937.....14-C3
Wyatt.....27-C8
Yadkin.....28-F1
Yadkin College.....28-D1
Yadkin Valley.....5-B8
Yadkinville • 2,525.....6-B3
Yale.....24-B3
Yanceyville • 1,973.....7-A6
Yaupon Beach 734.....14-D2
Yeatesville.....9-C5
Yellow Creek.....22-F1
Youngsville 424..7-B8,27-B8
Zebulon 3,173.....8-C1
Zephyr.....6-A2
Zirconia.....24-C4

SOUTH CAROLINA

Pop. (1990) 3,486,703
Area 31,055 Sq. Mi.

COUNTIES

County	County Seat	County	County Seat
Abbeville	Abbeville	Greenwood	Greenwood
Aiken	Aiken	Hampton	Hampton
Allendale	Allendale	Horry	Conway
Anderson	Anderson	Jasper	Ridgeland
Bamberg	Bamberg	Kershaw	Camden
Barnwell	Barnwell	Lancaster	Lancaster
Beaufort	Beaufort	Laurens	Laurens
Berkeley	Moncks Corner	Lee	Bishopville
Calhoun	St. Matthews	Lexington	Lexington
Charleston	Charleston	Marion	Marion
Cherokee	Chester	Marlboro	Bennettsville
Chesterfield	Chesterfield	McCormick	McCormick
Clarendon	Manning	Newberry	Newberry
Colleton	Walterboro	Oconee	Wahlahalla
Darlington	Darlington	Orangeburg	Orangeburg
Dillon	Dillon	Pickens	Pickens
Dorchester	St. George	Richland	Columbia
Edgefield	Edgefield	Saluda	Saluda
Fairfield	Winnsboro	Spartanburg	Spartanburg
Florence	Florence	Sumter	Sumter
Georgetown	Georgetown	Union	Union
Greenville	Greenville	Williamsburg	Kingstree
		York	York

COMPLETE LIST OF

CITIES AND TOWNS

1990 Census
• County Seats

Abbeville • 5,778.....11-C6
Adamsburg.....11-A8
Adams Run.....17-C5
Aiken •
19,872.....16-A2,18-E4
Alcolu.....12-D4
Alcot.....12-C4
Allendale • 4,410.....16-B3
Allsbrook.....13-C7
Almeda.....16-B3
Alvin.....17-A6
Anderson •
26,184.....11-B5,18-B2
Andrews 3,050.....17-A7
Angelus.....12-B3
Antreville.....11-C5
Appleton.....16-B3
Arcadia.....30-E1
Arcadia Lakes 899.....21-B8
Arial.....11-A5
Ashepoo.....17-C5
Ashland.....12-C4
Ashton.....16-B4
Ashwood.....12-C4
Atlantic
Beach 446.....13-D7,23-C6
Auburn.....12-B4
Awendaw.....17-B7
Aynor 470.....13-C6
Badham.....16-B4
Baldock.....16-B2
Ballentine.....12-C1
Bamberg • 3,843.....16-A3
Bannockburn.....13-C5,22-B4
Barksdale.....11-B6
Barnwell • 5,255.....16-A3
Barr.....12-D1
Barrelville.....17-C5
Barton.....16-B3
Batesburg 4,082.....11-D8
Batesville.....24-F3
Bath.....16-A1,18-E2
Baton Rouge.....11-B8
Bayboro.....13-C7
Beach Island.....18-F2
Beaufort • 9,576.....16-C4
Beech Island.....16-A1
Belton 4,646.....11-B5
Belvedere.....18-D2
Bennetts Point.....17-C5
Bennettsville • 9,345..13-B5
Bethany.....11-A8
Bethera.....17-B7
Bethune 405.....12-B3
Bingham.....13-B5
Bishopville • 3,560.....12-C4
Blacksburg 1,907.....11-A8
Blackstock.....12-B1
Blacksville 2,688.....16-A3
Blenheim 191.....13-B5
Bloomville.....12-D4
Blossom.....13-C5
Bluffton 738.....16-D4,25-B7
Blythewood 164.....12-C2
Boiling Springs.....11-A7
Bolentown.....16-A3
Bonham.....11-B7
Bonneau 374.....17-A6
Bowling Green.....12-A1
Bowman 1,063.....16-A4
Boyden.....21-E8
Boyden Arbor.....21-C8
Boykin.....12-C3
Bradley.....11-C6
Branchville 1,107.....16-A4
Briarcliffe Acres 552...13-D7
Brighton.....16-C3
Brighton Beach.....25-B7
Brogden.....12-D4
Brownsville.....13-B5
Brunson 587.....16-B3
Bucksport.....13-D7
Buffalo.....11-B7
Bullock Creek.....11-A8
Burgess.....13-D7
Burton.....16-C4
Byrds.....17-B5
Cades.....13-D5
Caesars Head.....11-A5
Cainhoy.....19-C8
Calhoun Falls 2,328.....11-C5
Callison.....11-C6
Calvin.....17-A7
Camden • 6,696.....12-C3
Cameron 504.....16-A4
Campfield.....17-A8
Campobello 465.....11-A6
Canadys.....16-B4
Carem.....11-B8
Carlisle 470.....11-B8
Cartersville.....12-C4
Cashville.....11-A6
Cassatt.....12-C3
Catawba.....12-A2
Cateechee.....11-A5
Cave.....16-B3
Cayce 11,163.....12-C2,21-E6
Centenary.....13-C6
Central 2,438.....11-A5
Chapin 282.....11-C8
Chappells 45.....11-C7
Charleston •
80,414.....17-C6,19-D5
Cheddar.....11-B5
Cheraw 5,505.....13-B5
Cherokee Falls.....11-A8
Cherokee Springs.....11-A7
Cherry Point.....16-D4
Chesnee 1,280.....11-A7
Chester • 7,158.....12-B1
Chesterfield • 1,373...12-B4
Chicora.....17-A6
City View 1,490.....24-D1
Clarks Hill.....11-D6
Claussen.....13-C5
Clearwater.....16-A1,18-E2
Clemson 11,096.....10-B4
Cleora.....11-D6
Cleveland.....11-A5
Clinton 7,987.....11-B7
Clio 882.....13-B5
Clover 3,422.....12-A1
Cokesbury.....11-C6
Colliers.....11-D6
Columbia •
98,052.....12-C2,21-C7
Conestee.....11-B6
Congaree.....12-D2
Converse.....11-A7
Conway • 9,819.....13-D7
Cool Spring.....13-C6
Cooper.....13-D5
Coosawhatchie.....16-C4
Cope 124.....16-A3
Cordesville.....17-B6
Cordova 135.....16-A4
Cornwell.....12-B1
Coronaca.....11-C6
Cottageville 572.....17-B5
Couchtown.....16-A2
Country Club
Estates.....30-C1
Coward 532.....13-C5
Cowpens 2,176.....11-A7
Creston.....16-A4
Crocketville.....16-B3
Cross.....17-A6
Cross Anchor.....11-B7
Cross Hill 469.....11-C7
Cross Keys.....11-B7
Cummings.....16-C3
Dacusville.....11-A5
Dale.....16-C4
Dalzell.....12-C3
Darlington • 7,311.....13-C5
Davidson.....16-C4
Davis Station....12-D4,17-A5
DeKalb.....12-B3
Denmark 3,762.....16-A3
Dentsville.....21-B8
Dillon • 6,829.....13-B6
Donalds 326.....11-B6
Dongola.....13-D6
Dorchester.....17-B5
Due West 1,220.....11-C6
Dukes.....16-B3
Dunbar.....13-B5
Duncan 2,152.....11-A6
Dyson.....11-C7
Eadytown.....17-A6
Earle.....17-A7
Early Branch.....16-C4
Easley 15,195.....11-A5
Eastatoe.....10-A4
Eastover 1,044.....12-D3
Ebenezer.....22-B3
Edgefield • 2,563.....11-D6
Edgemoor.....12-A2
Edisto Beach 340.....17-C5
Edisto Island.....17-C5
Edmund.....12-D1
Effingham.....13-C5
Ehrhardt 442.....16-B3
Elgin.....12-B2
Elgin 622.....12-C2
Elko 214.....16-A2
Elliott.....12-C4
Elloree 939.....17-A5
Enoree.....11-B7
Epworth.....11-C6
Estill 2,387.....16-C3
Eureka.....11-D7
Eutawville 350.....17-A5
Evergreen.....13-C5
Fairfax 2,317.....16-B3
Fairforest.....30-E1
Fairview
Cross Roads.....11-D8
Filbert.....12-A1
Fingerville.....11-A7
Fletcher.....13-B5
Florence •
29,813.....13-C5,22-B4
Floyd.....13-B5
Floydale.....13-C6
Floyds.....13-C7
Folly Beach
1,398.....17-C6,19-F6
Fords.....16-C3
Forest Acres
7,197.....12-C2,21-C7
Foreston.....12-D4,17-A6
Fork.....13-C6
Fork Shoals.....11-B6
Fort Fremont.....16-D4
Fort Lawn 718.....12-B2
Fort Mill 4,930.....12-A2
Fort Motte.....12-D3
Foster.....12-B4
Fountain Inn 4,388.....11-B6
Fowler.....13-D5
Furman 260.....16-C3
Gable.....12-D4
Gadsden.....12-D2
Gaffney • 13,145.....11-A7
Galivants Ferry.....13-C6
Gantt.....24-F1
Garden City.....13-D7,23-C8
Gardens Corner.....16-C4
Garnett.....16-C3
Gaston 984.....12-D2
Georgetown • 9,517...17-A8
Gifford 313.....16-B3
Gilbert 324.....11-D8
Gillisonville.....16-C3
Givhans.....17-B5
Glendale.....11-A7
Glen Springs.....11-A7
Gloverville.....16-A1,18-E3
Gluck.....11-B5
Glymphville.....11-B8
Goose Creek
24,692.....17-B6,19-A7
Gough.....17-B6
Gourdin.....17-A6
Govan 84.....16-B3
Gowensville.....11-A6
Grahamville.....16-C4
Gramling.....11-A6
Graniteville.....16-A1,18-E3
Gray Court 914.....11-B6
Grays.....16-C3
Great Falls 2,307.....12-B2
Greeleyville 464.....17-A6
Green Pond.....16-C4
Green Sea.....13-C7
Greenville •
58,282.....11-A6,24-F2
Greenwood • 20,807..11-C6
Greer 10,322.....11-A6,24-D4
Gresham.....13-D6
Grover.....16-B4
Hagood.....12-C3
Hamer.....13-B6
Hampton • 2,997.....16-B3
Hanahan
13,176.....17-B6,19-B6
Hancock.....12-A2
Hannah.....13-D5
Hardeeville 1,583.....16-D3
Harleyville 633.....17-B5
Hartsville 8,372.....12-B4
Heath Springs 907.....12-B3
Heineman.....12-D4,17-A6
Hemingway 829.....13-D6
Hendersonville.....16-C4
Henry.....13-D6
Hickory Grove 287.....11-A8
Hickory Grove.....13-D7
Hickory Tavern.....11-B6
Hilda 342.....16-A3
Hilton Head Island
23,694.....16-D4,25-B8
Hiotts.....17-B5
Hodges 125.....11-C6
Holly Hill 1,478.....17-A5
Hollywood 2,094.....17-C5
Homewood.....13-D7
Honea Path 3,841.....11-B6
Honey Hill.....17-B7
Horatio.....12-C3
Horrell Hill.....12-C2
Horry.....13-C6
Horrytown.....13-C7
Howard.....13-C7
Huger.....17-B6
Hyman.....13-C5
Indiantown.....13-D5
Inman 1,742.....11-A6
Irmo 11,280.....12-C1
Islandton.....16-B4
Isle of Palms
3,680.....17-C7,19-E8
Iva 1,174.....11-C5
Jackson 1,681.....16-A1
Jacksonboro.....17-C5
Jalapa.....11-C7
James Island...17-C6,19-E6
Jamestown 84.....17-A7
Jamison.....16-A4
Jedburg.....17-B5
Jefferson 745.....12-B3
Jenkinsville.....12-C1
Jennys.....16-B3
Joanna.....11-B7
Johns Island.....17-C6
Johnsonville 1,415.....13-D6
Johnston 2,688.....11-D7
Jonesville 1,205.....11-A7
Jordan.....12-D4,17-A5
Jordanville.....13-D6
Kathwood.....16-A1
Kemper.....13-C6
Kershaw 1,814.....12-B3
Killian.....12-C2
Kinards.....11-B7
Kingsburg.....13-D6
Kings Creek.....11-A8
Kingstree • 3,858.....13-D5
Kirksey.....11-C6
Kitchings Mill.....16-A2
Kline 285.....16-B3
Kneece.....11-D8
La France.....11-B5
Lake City 7,153.....13-D5
Lake View 872.....13-C6
Lakewood.....23-B7
Lamar 1,125.....12-C4
Lancaster • 8,914.....12-B2
Lando.....12-B2
Landrum 2,347.....11-A6
Lanford.....11-B7
Langley.....18-E3
Latta 1,565.....13-C6
Laurel.....23-E7
Laurel Bay.....16-C4
Laurens • 9,694.....11-B6
Leeds.....11-B8
Lees.....16-A3
Leesville 2,025.....11-D8
Lesslie.....12-A2
Lewis.....12-B1
Lexington • 3,289.....12-C1
Liberty 3,228.....11-A5
Liberty Hill.....12-B2
Litchfield
Beach.....17-A8,23-E8
Little Mountain 235.....11-C8
Little River.....13-D8,23-A6
Little Rock.....13-B6
Livingston 171.....16-A3
Lobeco.....16-C4
Lockhart 58.....11-B8
Lodge 147.....16-B4
Lone Star.....12-D3
Longcreek.....10-A3
Longs.....13-C7
Longtown.....12-C2
Loris 2,067.....13-C7
Lowndesville 162.....11-C5
Lowrys 200.....12-A1
Lugoff.....12-C3
Luray 102.....16-B3
Lydia.....12-C4
Lykesland.....12-D2
Lyman 2,271.....11-A6
Lynchburg 475.....12-C4
Lyndhurst.....16-B2
Maddens.....11-B6
Madison.....10-B3
Manning • 4,428.....12-D4
Manville.....12-C4
Marietta.....11-A5
Marion • 7,658.....13-C6
Marlboro.....13-B5
Mars Bluff.....13-C5
Martin.....16-B2
Mary.....13-D7
Mauldin 11,587..11-A6,24-F2
May.....11-A7
Mayesville 694.....12-C4
Mayson.....11-C7
McBee 715.....12-B4
McClellanville 333.....17-B7
McColl 2,685.....13-B5
McConnells 157.....12-A1
McCormick • 1,659.....11-D6
Mechanicsville.....13-C5
Meggett 787.....17-C5
Meriwether.....11-D6
Midway.....16-A4
Miley.....16-B3
Millett.....16-B2
Mitford.....12-B2
Modoc.....11-D6
Monarch.....11-B7
Moncks
Corner • 5,607.....17-B6
Monetta 285.....11-D7
Montclare.....13-B5
Monticello.....12-C1
Montmorenci.....16-A2
Moore.....11-A7
Mountain Rest.....10-A4
Mount Carmel 117.....11-C5
Mount Croghan 131.....12-B4
Mount Holly.....17-B6
Mount Pleasant
30,108.....17-C6,19-D7
Mountville.....11-B7
Mount Willing.....11-C7
Mouzon.....12-D4
Mullins 5,910.....13-C6
Murrells Inlet....13-D7,23-D8
Myrtle Beach
24,848.....13-D7,23-E5
Myrtle Island.....25-B7
Neeses 410.....16-A3
Nesmith.....13-D6
Newberry • 10,542.....11-C7
New Ellenton 2,515.....16-A2
New Holland.....11-D8
New Market.....11-C6
New Morrisville.....17-A7
Newport.....12-A2,30-A1
New Prospect.....11-A6
Newry.....10-B4
New Zion.....12-D4
Nichols 528.....13-C6
Ninety Six 2,099.....11-C6
Nixons Cross
Roads.....13-D8,23-B5
Nixonville.....13-D7
Norris 884.....11-B5
North 809.....16-A3
North Augusta
15,351.....16-A1,18-D1
North Charleston
70,218.....17-B6,19-A6
North Litchfield
Beach.....23-E8
North Myrtle
Beach 8,636.13-D8,23-B5
Norway 401.....16-A3
Oak Grove.....13-C5
Oakley.....17-B6
Oakway.....10-B4
Oakwood.....16-A2
Oatland.....17-A8
Oats.....12-C4
Ogden.....12-A2
Olanta 687.....12-D4
Olar 391.....16-B3
Old House.....16-C4
Orangeburg • 13,739..16-A4
Orum.....13-C5
Osborn.....17-C5
Oswego.....12-C4
Outland.....13-D6
Owdoms.....11-C7
Owings.....11-B6
Pacolet 1,736.....11-A7
Pacolet Mills 696.....11-A7
Padgett.....16-B4
Pageland 2,666.....12-B3
Palmetto.....13-C5,22-A3
Pamplico 1,314.....13-C5
Panola.....12-D3
Paris.....11-A6,24-D2
Parkers Ferry.....17-C5
Parksville 193.....11-D6
Parler.....17-A5
Patrick 368.....12-B4
Pauline.....11-A7
Pawleys
Island 176...17-A8,23-F8
Paxville 218.....12-D3
Peak 78.....12-C1
Pee Dee.....13-C5
Pelham.....11-A6,24-F4
Pelion 336.....12-D1
Pelzer 81.....11-B5
Pendleton 3,314.....11-B5
Perry 241.....16-A3
Pickens • 3,042.....11-A5
Piedmont.....11-B5
Pine Island.....13-D7
Pineland.....16-C3
Pine Ridge 1,731.....21-F5
Pineville.....17-A6
Pinewood 600.....12-D3
Pinopolis.....17-A6
Plantersville.....17-A8
Pleasant Hill.....12-B3
Pleasant Lane.....11-D6
Plum Branch 101.....11-D6
Pocotaligo.....16-C4
Polk.....18-D4
Pomaria 267.....11-C8
Pontiac.....12-C2
Port Royal 2,985.....16-C4
Pregnall.....17-B5
Primus.....12-B3
Princeton.....11-B6
Pritchardville.....16-D3
Prosperity 1,116.....11-C8
Pumpkintown.....11-A5
Purdy.....13-D6
Purysburgh Landing...16-D3
Quinby 865.....22-A4
Rains.....13-C6
Rantowles.....17-C6
Ravenel 2,165.....17-C5
Red Bank.....12-D1
Red Bluff Crossroads..13-D7
Reevesville 244.....16-B4
Reidville.....11-A6
Rembert.....12-C3
Rhems.....17-A7
Richburg 405.....12-B2
Richland.....10-B4
Ridgeland • 1,071.....16-C3
Ridge Spring 861.....11-D7
Ridgeville 1,625.....17-B5
Ridgeway 407.....12-C2
Riley.....16-A4
Rimini.....12-D3
Rion.....12-C1
Ritter.....16-C4
Robertville.....16-C3
Rock Hill
41,643.....12-A2,30-B2
Rockton.....12-C2
Rockville.....17-C5
Rocky Bottom.....11-A5
Rodman.....12-B2
Roebuck.....11-A7
Rosinville.....17-A5
Round.....17-B5
Rowesville 316.....16-A4
Ruby 300.....12-B4
Ruffin.....16-B4
Russellville.....17-A6
St. Andrews.....19-D6
St. Charles.....12-C4
St. George • 2,077.....17-B5
St. Matthews • 2,345..12-D2
St. Paul.....17-A5
St. Stephen.....17-A6
Salak.....11-C6
Salem 192.....10-A4
Salley 451.....16-A3
Salters.....13-D5
Saluca.....11-C6
Saluda • 2,798.....11-C7
Sampit.....17-A7
Sandy Run.....12-D2
Santee 638.....17-A5
Santuck.....11-
Sardinia.....12-D
Sardis.....12-C
Scotia 182.....16-C
Scranton 802.....13-D
Sedalia.....11-B
Seigling.....16-
Sellers 358.....13-C
Seneca 7,726.....10-B
Shannontown.....12-D
Sharon 270.....11-A
Sheldon.....16-C
Shell.....13-D
Shelton.....11-B
Shiloh.....12-D
Shirley.....16-C
Shoals Junction.....11-B
Shulerville.....17-B
Sidney.....17-B
Silver.....12-C
Silvertreet 156.....11-C
Simpson 11,708.....12-C
Simpsonville.....11-B
Smallwood.....12-C
Smithboro.....13-C
Smith Turn Out.....12-A
Smoaks 142.....16-B
Smyrna 57.....11-A
Snelling 125.....16-A
Snowden.....19-D
Socastee.....13-D
Society Hill 686.....13-B
South
Congaree 2,406.....21-F
South Lynchburg.....12-C
Sparrows.....13-C
Spartanburg •
43,467.....11-A7,30-F
Springdale
3,226.....12-D2,21-E
Springfield 523.....16-A
Starr 164.....11-B
Stateburg.....12-C
Steedman.....11-D
Stilton.....16-A
Stoneboro.....12-B
Strother.....11-B
Sullivans
Island 1,623..17-C6,19-E
Summerton 975.....12-A
Summerville 22,519...17-B
Sumter • 41,943.....12-D
Sunset.....11-A
Surfside
Beach 3,845.13-D7,23-B
Swansea 527.....12-D
Switzer.....11-A
Switzerland.....16-C
Sycamore 208.....16-B
Tamassee.....10-A
Tarboro.....16-C
Tatum 49.....13-B
Taxahaw.....12-B
Taylor.....11-A6,24-D
Tega Cay 3,016.....12-A
Thicketty.....11-A
Tigerville.....11-A
Tilman.....16-C
Timmonsville 2,182.....12-C
Toddville.....13-D
Tokeena.....10-B
Townville.....10-B
Tradesville.....12-B
Travelers Rest 3,069..11-A
Trenton 303.....11-D
Trio.....17-A
Troy 140.....11-C
Tulie.....30-F
Turberville 698.....12-D
Ulmer 90.....16-B
Union • 9,836.....11-B
Union Cross Roads.....13-D
Ute.....24-D
Vance 214.....17-A
Van Wyckz.....12-A
Varnville 1,970.....16-B
Vaucluse.....16-A1,18-D
Verdery.....11-C
Wagener 731.....11-D
Walhalla • 3,755.....10-A
Wallace.....13-B
Walterboro • 5,492.....16-B
Wampee.....13-D7,23-B
Wando.....17-B
Ward 132.....11-D
Ware Shoals 2,497.....11-B
Warrenville.....16-A1,18-E
Warsaw.....17-A
Wateree.....12-D
Waterloo 122.....11-C
Watts Mills.....11-B
Waverly Mills.....23-F
Wedgefield.....12-D
West Columbia
10,588.....12-C2,21-C
Westminster 3,120.....10-B
West Springs.....11-B
West Union 260.....10-A
Westville.....12-B
White Hall.....16-C
White Oak.....12-B
White Pond.....16-A
White Rock.....12-C
Whitmire 1,702.....11-B
Wiggins.....17-C
Wilder.....17-A
Wilkins.....16-C
Wilkinsville.....11-A
Williams 188.....16-B
Williamston 3,876.....11-B
Willington.....11-C
Williston 3,099.....16-A
Wilson.....12-D
Windsor 124.....16-A
Winnsboro • 3,475.....12-B
Wisacky.....12-C
Wolfton.....16-A
Woodford 200.....12-D
Woodrow 4,365.....12-C
Woodruff.....11-B
Woodward.....12-B
Yauhannah.....13-D
Yemassee 728.....16-C
Yenome.....16-B
Yonges Island.....17-C
York • 6,709.....12-A
Zion.....13-C

NA-682-J-

The CAROLINAS

CONTENTS

TEXT ❧ MARY T. MULKERIN

DESIGN ❧ EDWARD P. O'DELL

NORTH CAROLINA

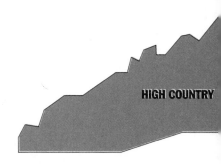

HIGH COUNTRY

The story of North Carolina begins in 1597 when the first English settlers arrived near Roanoke Island. It was among this group that the first American child of English parents, Virginia Dare, was born. However, what happened to Virginia, her parents and the rest of the settlement remains a riddle. The entire community disappeared leaving the word "CRAOTOAN" etched crudely into a tree. Historians believe that this may have referred to the Craotan Indians, a friendly tribe who lived nearby. Whether the settlers were killed by the Indians or were absorbed into their culture remains one of our nation's earliest and most puzzling mysteries.

North Carolinians have always been a free-thinking, democratic and spirited group. Though relatively few battles of the American Revolution were fought here, England's General Cornwallis met plenty of resistance. Several battles, such as the Battle of Guilford Courthouse, were technical victories for the Red Coats but were later categorized by historians as strategic turning points for the Americans.

Later, the Civil War divided factions within the state. Western residents were solidly Union while southern inhabitants were for the Confederacy. As a state, North Carolina did not officially join the Confederates until Fort Sumter was fired upon in 1861. Once committed, however,

the state furnished fully one-fifth of the Confederate Army. It was also during the Civil War that North Carolina earned its enduring nickname: The Tar Heel State. For the most of the 19th century, North Carolina produced large quantities of tar and turpentine. Legend has it that General Robert E. Lee christened the troops from North Carolina the "Tar Heel Boys" because they were well-known for sticking so long in battle. Lee felt that troops from other states could have used a little tar on their heels as well.

North Carolina had a tough time recovering during Reconstruction. However, since free Blacks had been accepted since 1860, the state had an easier time adjusting to life without slavery than many other southern states. Industrial plants and textile mills sprang up along some of the more powerful rivers, and many of the state's colleges and universities became the best in the South.

Today North Carolina is well-loved for its beauty. "For purple mountains majesty..." perfectly describes the breathtaking views along the Blue Ridge Parkway while the beaches along the coast and Outer Banks are among the finest in the nation. Golf enthusiasts flock to North Carolina from all over the country, and fishing in everything, from the tiniest creeks to the Atlantic Ocean, is another favorite pastime. Whatever you enjoy, you're sure to find it in North Carolina, the state that bills itself "Variety Vacationland."

Exploring the Regions of North Carolina

North Carolina is comprised of three distinct geographic regions, all of which work together to form one great state. The largest area of the state is the Piedmont Plateau, the thriving center of North Carolina where many of the largest cities and much of the best golfing in the state, (some say the country), can be found. East of the Piedmont region lie the Coastal Plains which reach from the Outer Banks, a string of barrier islands over 100 miles long, to well inland. To the west of the Piedmont Plateau is the moutainous High Country. Individually each region is spectacular, but combined they result in a unique state that is becoming ever more popular to live in and has always been a treat to visit.

The High Country

The High Country of North Carolina, sometimes called the "Land of the Sky," is most simply described by that overworked word, majestic. The mountains of North Carolina are older that both the Andes and the Alps and are as beautiful

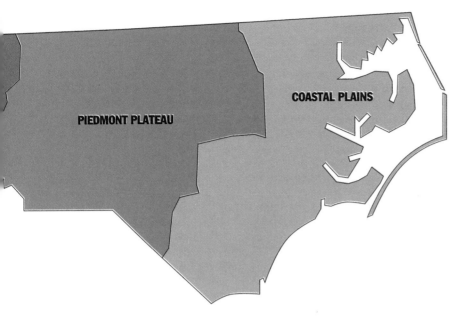

PIEDMONT PLATEAU

COASTAL PLAINS

as any mountains in the world. Experiencing nature's wonders is as easy as taking a drive along the Blue Ridge Parkway or as challenging as exploring the Great Smoky Mountains with nothing but a backpack and a water bottle. The serene rolling pastures and dramatic waterfalls of the region are as impressive as its highest mountain tops. As a result much of the High Country is preserved as state and national parks.

Despite its startling beauty, a physical description of the High Country only begins to tell the story of the mountains of North Carolina. Besides the richness of the land, there is a richness in the people and their heritage that shines through as you get to know the area. Here, life is a little slower and people take pride in their work and their way of life. Whether it's rock candy from an old-fashioned general store or a homemade quilt, you'll want to take some of the High Country home with you.

Attractions

Cowee Valley Mines in Franklin was once mined commercially by Tiffany's and the like. More that 30 distinct mineral crystals may be found in area mines including rubies, sapphires, rodolites, garnets, quartz and others. Rushing mountain streams washed precious and semi-precious stones to the valley below. Though the conglomerates have

abandoned this area, amateurs are invited for "rock-hounding." (800) 336-7829. [p.22,F-3]

The Appalachian Cultural Museum in Boone is devoted to the culture and history of the Blue Ridge Mountains. Exhibits include tools, artifacts, Winston Cup race cars, and dioramas. (704) 262-3117. [p.5,B-7]

The Cherokee Indian Reservation in Qualla Boundary [see map p.22] is home to the eastern band of the Cherokee Indians. The 56,000-acre tract contains various points of interest including the Museum of the Cherokee Indian [p.22, E-3] which honors the culture and history of the Cherokee. Oconaluftee Indian Village [p.22, E-3] is a faithful recreation of an ancient Cherokee community. (704) 497-2771.

The Folk Art Center on the Blue Ridge Parkway east of Asheville is a cooperative project between the Southern Highland Handicraft Guild and the National Park Service. Works are displayed, skills are demonstrated and many unusual and well-made items are for sale. (704) 298-7928. [p.18, B-4]

The Tweetsie Railroad, an amusement park in Blowing Rock, has a steam locomotive that transports passengers through narrow mountain passes and an authentic frontier village. (704) 264-9061. [p.5, B-8]

The Piedmont Plateau

The Piedmont Plateau, the largest region in the state, occupies the area between the High Country mountains and the Coastal Plains. Unlike the state's other two regions, the Piedmont area is more accurately described by its varied activity rather than its less distinctive terrain. Sometimes called the Heartland, this area contains the state's largest cities, biggest industries and some of the best universities in the South; a few are among the best in the nation.

In the area east of the great mountains you'll find an abundance of lakes and rivers with factories and industrial plants scattered among them. The Stroh's Brewery is here and North Carolina is world famous for her fine furniture-making factories. In fact, bargain hunters and newlyweds setting up house often travel to the furniture outlets in this part of North Carolina for some of the best-made pieces at the best prices. Some of the finest pottery in the world is crafted here as well. Buyers are invariably delighted with their purchases and hope that some of the better, signed pieces may become collector's items some day.

The modern cities of Charlotte and Raleigh (described in detail in a later section) are busy centers of business and culture. They are consistently rated among the nation's most livable cities and are a charming blend of yesterday and tomorrow. Though they each have many of the advantages and some of the disadvantages of a large city, they retain a home-town flavor and are best termed "little-big cities." Each has its own collection of fine museums, centers for the performing arts, institutions of higher learning as well as first-class hotels and four-star restaurants.

Some of the finest golf courses in the country are located in the lower Piedmont. The World Golf Hall of Fame [p.7, D-6] is here as are several PGA Tour courses. Tanglewood Park is one of the top 25 public golf courses in the country. In the Piedmont, there's every opportunity to work hard and play harder.

Attractions

82 Airborne Division Museum near Fayetteville illustrates the history of the nation's first airborne division and is located on the 200 square mile army base, Fort Bragg. (919) 432-5307. [p.7, D-7]

Belmont Abbey Cathedral in Belmont was completed in 1894 and between 1910 and 1977 was the only Abbey Cathedral in the country. Part of a Benedictine Monastery, the Gothic-style cathedral was constructed of bricks that were hand-made by monks from local clay.(704) 825-6890. [p.20, C-2]

Bentonville Battleground State Historic Site in Johnson County is where the biggest Civil War battle fought on North Carolina soil took place. Here, Confederate forces staged their most ambitious attempt at stopping Sherman's advance north from Savannah. Harper House, a former field hospital, has been restored. (919) 594-0789 [p.8, D-1]

Cannon Mills Visitor Center in Kanapolis is a curious place to visit if you're interested in the textile industry and its evolution in the Piedmont. Tours of Cannon, a leading manufacturer of sheets and towels, are available and are highlighted by a demonstration of the latest weaving techniques. Be sure to visit the factory outlet for discounts of up to 70 percent. Reservations required; no children under 16 years old. (704) 938-3200. [p.20, A-4]

Korner's Folly in Kernersville is one of the region's most unusual attractions. Built in 1880, the 22-room house was constructed on seven levels. The top floor was renovated in 1897 as the first "Little Theater" in the nation. (919) 993-4521. [p.28, B-4]

North Carolina Zoological Park in Asheboro is a unique concept in zoos. Even if you don't like zoos, this one should not be missed. At 1,300 acres, it's the largest natural habitat zoo in the world. The environments of the major continents have been recreated with exhibits of the wild life that is indigenous to them. (919) 879-7000. [p.7, C-5]

Reed Gold Mine State Historic Site near Concord was the country's first gold mine. It was here in 1799 that a young man named Conrad Reed found a nugget of pure gold. Visitors can tour the mine's underground tunnels, observe an ore-

crushing mill and pan for gold themselves. (704) 786-8337. [p.6, D-3]

Stroh Brewery Company near Winston-Salem provides over 4 million barrels of beer each year and is one of the largest manufacturing plants under one roof in North Carolina. (919) 788-6710. [p.28, C-2]

The National Railroad Museum is located in Hamlet, which was once a major center of railroad activity. The old depot, now on the National Register of Historic Places, houses the main body of the museum and contains railroad memorabilia and equipment along with rare maps and photographs. (919) 895-9058. [p.13, A-5]

The Coastal Plains

Eventually the sandhills and red clay of the Piedmont give way to the Coastal Plains. The coast itself varies in character from the quiet beauty of Nags Head and the serenity of Cape Hatteras National Seashore to the bustling seaport of Wilmington. Along the coast you can find secret coves, unusual marine life, fertile swamplands and lush woods. Solitary lighthouses punctuating the shore can lead you from the famous Outer Banks to more remote towns like Duck and Corolla. In fact, since much of the central North Carolina coast is protected as National Seashore, lighthouses are about the only man-made structures you'll see.

The North Carolina coast is also alive with history. It was here that two brothers named Wright started what was to become phenomenon, an industry and a science: aviation. It was here, also, that centuries earlier English pioneers arrived almost 40 years before the settlement at Plymouth Rock. The Elizabethan adventurers vanished and their disappearance is still one of our nation's oldest and most perplexing mysteries.

To get the most from the North Carolina coast, enjoy the sun, sea and sand and all that nature provides. But do take a moment to appreciate some of the events that occurred along these shores, events that helped to shape a nation.

Attractions

Historic Bath was incorporated in 1705

and is the oldest chartered settlement in North Carolina. Many surviving structures from the 18th and 19th centuries have been restored and are opened to the public. Palmer-Marsh House, with its famed double chimney, is one of the oldest homes in the state and is a national Historical Landmark. Saint Thomas Church is the oldest church in the state. While here, don't miss the Banner House and the Van Der Veer House. (919) 923-3971. [p.9, C-5]

Historic New Bern contains over 150 landmarks and structures listed on the National Register of Historic Places. New Bern was once North Carolina's state capital. The best way to make sure you see it all is to stop by the Visitor's Center for maps and cassette tapes for self-guided tours. (800) 437-5767. [See map p.25.]

Historic Wilmington has always been a very busy port in North Carolina. There are many attractions in this lively seaport town including the Burgwin-Wright House, Wilmington Railroad Museum, Chandler's Wharf and the Governor Dudley Mansion. (919) 341-4030 [p.30, E-3]

Ocracoke Village on Ocracoke Island is where famed pirate Blackbeard (Edward Teach) was slain. Many believe his treasure is still buried beneath this charming island community. (919) 928-4531. [p.9, D-7]

Wright Brothers National Monument near Kitty Hawk contains a visitor's center, museum and an airstrip. All mark the spot where Wilbur and Orville Wright made the world's first powered aircraft flight on December 17, 1903. It can get very windy here which is the reason the two brothers from Ohio came so far to try their "outrageous" experiment. (919) 441-7430. [p.9, B-8]

USS North Carolina Battleship Memorial in Wilmington is a museum and memorial to all veterans of World War II. Commissioned in 1941, it was America's first modern battleship. During the summer, don't miss "Immortal Showboat," a spectacular sound and light show presented at the ship. (919) 251-5805. [p.30, E-3]

CITY LIGHTS

IN NORTH CAROLINA

*The cities of North Carolina
are where business is conducted,
where large numbers of students are educated
and where state laws are effected. By general
standards, some of North Carolina's cities
are fairly large while others are quite small.
Each, as you'll discover, is unique
in its own way.*

*This section highlights the
five major cities in North Carolina,
focusing on the history, character
and attractions of each.*

ASHEVILLE

Asheville [see map p.18] was settled almost 200 years ago, in 1797, as a tiny trading outpost deep in the mountains of western North Carolina near the Tennessee border. Since then, the city and its environs have grown to become a world-class resort destination, a community that still retains the magical essence of the past while keeping in touch with our ever-changing present.

Aside from its magnificent setting in the Blue Ridge Mountains and its proximity to the Great Smoky Mountains, Asheville is also well-known for its grab-bag collection of unusual architecture. Downtown Asheville is like a museum, featuring buildings from the classical period through the contemporary. No tourist worth his salt could leave Asheville without learning about her two favorite sons: George Vanderbilt and Thomas Wolfe. Vanderbilt wasn't a native but chose Asheville as the setting for his magnificent estate, now a National Historic Landmark. Wolfe, who grew up in Asheville, immortalized the town in the novel *Look Homeward, Angel*, in which "Dixieland," featured so prominently in the book, was actually his mother's boarding house on Spruce Street. The house is still standing today. Wolfe is buried in Asheville along with another literary great, William Sydney Porter, more commonly known as O. Henry.

Though Asheville is a contemporary city, its still just a mountain village. You're just as likely to see modern artisans working at Appalachian lifestyle arts as you are to dance (or at least stomp your feet) to the strains of real country bluegrass. The riches of mountain life are well known and Asheville is voted, year after year, as one of the country's most livable cities–one visit and you'll know why.

CONTACT: Asheville Visitor Information Center, 151 Haywood St., (800) 257-1300, and Asheville Convention and Visitor's Bureau, Box 1010, 151 Haywood St., Asheville, NC 28802-1010, (704) 258-3858.

Attractions

Asheville Art Museum - One of five attractions of Park Place. The others are: The Health Adventure, Coburn Gem and Mineral Museum, YMI Cultural Center and the Diana Wortham Theater. Permanent collection and changing exhibits. (Park Place Education Arts and Science Center, 2 South Park Square, (704) 257-4500. Admission.) [p.18, B-3]

Biltmore Estate - The 250-room mansion on this 8,000-acre estate took one thousand men five years to build. The French Renaissance chateau was built as the private residence of George Vanderbilt and is now a museum whose art, priceless furnishings and formal gardens are absolutely magnificent. Sixty-five rooms are open to visitors as are 17 acres of gardens, and winery with free wine tasting. The self-guided tour takes about two hours but it's easy to stay all day! (Call (704) 255-1700 for directions. Daily 9am-5pm. Admission.) [p.18, B-3]

Downtown Asheville is noted for its eclectic architecture featuring neo-classical, baroque and art deco structures (and almost everything else in between.) Be sure to pick up a copy of "Asheville Urban Trail" from the Asheville Visitors Center [p.18, B-3] to guide you through the city's wealth of the architectural treasures. For group tours, call the Preservation Society of Asheville and Buncombe County, (704) 254-2343 for details.

The Homespun Shops - Not just a shopping area, as the name implies, but an old school founded almost a century ago by Mrs. Vanderbilt to keep the ancient skills of dyeing, spinning and weaving wool and cotton alive and profitable for hard-working artisans. Craft gallery, studios, museums and cafe. (Grovewood Avenue near Macon Avenue, (704) 253-7651, call for times.) [p.18, A-4]

Thomas Wolfe Memorial - One of the oldest buildings in downtown Asheville. Thomas Wolfe's mother ran this as a boarding house for years. The "Old Kentucky Home" as it is known in Asheville was immortalized as "Dixieland" in Wolfe's book *Look Homeward, Angel.* Now a State Historic Site, the house retains its origi-nal furnishings and photos belonging to the Wolfe family. (48 Spruce St. Hours vary throughout the year, call (704) 253-8304 for information. Admission.) [p.18, B-3]

Zebulon B. Vance Birthplace State Historic Site - Vance was North Carolina's governor during the Civil War. He and his family were deeply involved in the early history of the state and this park is a tribute to their dedication and accomplishments. The reconstructed log cabin is where Vance grew up. Picnic facilities are located on the grounds. (Reems Creek Road, Rt. 1103 about 6 miles from US 23 in Weaverville, Apr.-Oct., Mon-Sat 9-5, Sun 1-5; Nov.-March, Tue-Sat 9-4, Sun 10-4, (704) 645-6706. Free.) [p.5, C-5]

CHARLOTTE

Charlotte [see map p.20] is the most populous city in the Carolinas. Its function as a bold leader in the new south coupled with its spunky role in U.S. history makes it one of the more interesting cities in the state. Settled in the 1740's and incorporated in 1768, the town named itself after King George III's wife Queen Charlotte and the county, Mecklenburg, after her hometown in Germany. If affinity for the Queen was ever sincere, it was short lived: Lord Cornwallis was moved to remark during his brief occupation of the city that Charlotteans's patriotic actions reminded him of a "hornest's nest," a moniker that survives to this day.

Charlotte has always been strong economically. In 1836 the first branch of the U.S. Mint was opened. Gold had been discovered in 1799 and, until the California Gold Rush of 1849, Charlotte was the greatest gold producer in the country. After the Civil War and the abolition of slavery, Charlotte made an easy transition from an economy based on slave labor to one based upon industry. This was primarily due to the Catawba River and the tremendous water power it generated to fuel industrial plants and textile mills.

Today Charlotte is a sophisticated, progressive city poised to charge into the 21st century. Over 600 textile plants are located within a 100-mile radius. Its convenient location has enabled Charlotte to become one of the South's leaders in transportation, finance, education and medicine. The "Queen City" has a colorful history of strength and ingenuity, a tradition that continues to this day.

CONTACT: Charlotte Convention & Visitors Bureau, 122 E. Stonewall St. 28202-1838, (704) 334-2282.

Attractions:

Afro-American Cultural Center - This museum, built as Little Rock Ame Zion Church in 1911, is devoted to African American culture, history and art. Besides a permanent collection, there is a full calendar of events, lectures and performances. (401 N. Myers St. (704) 374-1565, Tue-Sat 10-6,Sun 1-5. Free.) [p.20, C-3]

Charlotte Motor Speedway - This is the country's premier NASCAR facility, home to the Coca-Cola 600, the longest stock car race in the world. The speedway also host the Winston, The Champion Spark Plug 300, the All Pro Auto Parts 300 and the Mello Yello 500 as well as many other races and the annual Auto Fairs. (Approx. 15 miles northeast of Charlotte on U.S. Highway 29, call (704) 455-3200 for tickets and schedule information.) [p.20, B-4]

Charlotte Museum of History and Hezekiah Alexander Homesite - The former residence of one of North Carolina's early settlers and signer of the Mecklenburg Declaration of Independence in 1775. This "rock house" is the oldest dwelling (1774) in Mecklenburg County. Guided tours are given of the homesite, spring house, herb garden and log kitchen. (3500 Shamrock Dr., Tue-Fri 10-5, Sat-Sun 2-5, (704) 374-1565. Admission.) [p.20, C-3]

Discovery Place - Award winning hands-on science and technology museum where visitors are encouraged to get involved. Special features include a rain forest, tidal pool, touch pool, aquarium, life center and changing science exhibits. (301 N Tryon St. Mon- Fri 9-5, Sat 9-6, Sun 1-6, (704) 372-6261 Admission.) [p.20, C-3]

Latta Place - This preserved river plantation, circa 1800, is in the Georgian/Federal style and features a slave house, barn, smokehouse, and cotton-field. It is located on Latta Plantation Park, a 1700 acre preserve on Mt. Island Lake featuring picnicking, hiking, canoeing, an equestrian center and a sanctuary for injured birds. (5225 Sample Rd., Huntersville, 12 miles north of uptown Charlotte. Park opens daily 7am-dark. Free. Tours of house 1:30 and 3:30pm Tue-Fri, 1:30, 2:30, 3:30 Sat and Sun. (704) 875-2312. Admission.) [p20, B-2]

James K. Polk Memorial - Our 11th President, James K. Polk, was born here in 1795. You can visit the reconstructed log home and its outbuilding. Visitors Center features exhibits, a film on Polk's life and career and guided tours. (14 miles south of uptown on Highway 521, Mon-Sat 9-5, Sun 1-5. (704) 889-7145. Free) [p.20, D-2]

Mint Museum of Art - From 1837-1861 and from 1867-1913 this building served as the First Branch U.S. Mint. Since 1933 it has been an art museum housing American, European, pre-Columbian and African art and artifacts. Also featured is a vast collection of porcelain, maps, period costumes and antique coins minted on the premises. (2730 Randolph Rd., Tue 10-10, Wed-Sat 10-5, Sun 1-6, (704) 337-2000. Admission.) [p.20, C-3]

Spirit Square Center for the Arts - Center for the visual and performing arts includes seven art galleries, three performance spaces and offers lectures and performances. Call for schedule information. (345 N. College St., Tue-Sat noon-6pm, later on performance evenings. (704) 372-9664.) [p.20 C-3]

University of North Carolina at Charlotte - UNCC is a lively campus but the main attraction is the spectacular landscaping and gardens. In April and May the rhododendron garden is magnificent. Also of interest are the ornamental garden, botanical gardens and public greenhouse. (8 miles north of uptown on Highway 4, (704) 547-2000.) [p.20, C-3]

RALEIGH • DURHAM • CHAPEL HILL

In 1792, Raleigh was declared by the General Assembly to be North Carolina's "unalterable seat of government." Today it's not only North Carolina's capital but also a center for research, industry and commerce and the base of the Triangle Area of Raleigh, Durham and Chapel Hill. [See maps p.26-27.]

Sir Walter Raleigh, after whom Raleigh is named, was a true Renaissance man: writer, statesman and an independent thinker. In many ways, it seems his spirited personality has influenced the city that bears his name. Six colleges are located in Raleigh and some of the south's finest institutions of higher learning are located in the Triangle Area. After surrendering to Sherman in 1865, state lawmakers voted themselves a raise, set up a bar in the state capital and permanently nicked the main steps by constantly rolling whiskey barrels up them. Even that temporary period as a government full of scalawags and carpetbaggers has done little to harm the modern day strength of one of North Carolina's most progressive cities.

Research Triangle Park, a 5,000-acre commercial area between the Triangle cities is dedicated to the advancement of science and research as it applies to industry, technology, the environment and government. A visit to Raleigh and the Triangle Area is likely to broaden the mind and raise more than a few questions, so enjoy.

CONTACT: Raleigh Convention and Visitors Bureau, 225 Hillsborough St., Suite 400, Box 1879, Raleigh, NC 27602-1879, (919) 834-5900.

Attractions: Raleigh

Executive Mansion - A fine example of Queen Anne cottage-style Victorian architecture, the mansion has been home to North Carolina's governors since 1891. It is constructed primarily of North Carolina materials and is one of the most beautiful attractions in Raleigh. (200 N. Blount St. Tours by appointment, (919) 733-3456. Free.) [p.27, E-7]

Historic Oakwood - Since 1977 many of the houses in Raleigh's most prestigious post Victorian neighborhood have been restored to their original state by their residents. A walk down these few blocks allows visitors to view some of the finest homes in Raleigh built during the late 18th and 19th centuries (Blount St. is just one street in this historic neighborhood NE of Downtown). [p.27, E-7]

Mordecai Historic Park - The location of Mordecai Plantation features the original plantation house built in 1785. The park includes several historic buildings including the birthplace of President Andrew Johnson. (1 Mimosa St. Open year-round Mon-Fri 10-3pm, Sat-Sun 1:30-3:30pm. (919) 834-4844. Admission. [p.27, E-7]

North Carolina Museum of Art - An internationally noted collection of European, American, Ancient, Judaic, African, New World, Oceanic, and 20th Century art and varied changing exhibits. (2110 Blue Ridge Road, Tue-Sat 9-5, Fri 9-9, Sun 11-6, (919) 833-1935. Tours daily at 1:30. Free.) [p.27, E-6]

North Carolina Museum of History - This is a great place to learn about North Carolina's history. The museum features over 100,000 artifacts depicting 400 years of the state's heritage with special emphasis on North Carolina folklife, women's and sports history. (1 East Edenton St, Tue-Sat 9-5, Sun 1-6, (919) 715-0200. Free.) [p.27, E-7]

North Carolina State Museum of Natural Sciences - Established in 1879, this museum has exhibits focusing on the state's biological and geological diversity with emphasis on fossils. (Bicentennial Plaza, Mon-Sat 9-5, Sun 1-5, (919) 733-7450. Free.) [p.27, E-7]

State Capitol - This Greek Revival building was completed in 1840, restored in 1976 and is a National Historic Landmark. Until 1888, it housed the governor's office, cabinet offices, library and legislative offices. Now most of those offices are located in the legislative building, but the restored legislative chambers as well as the offices of the governor and secretary of state remain. The Capitol Building is surrounded by an attractive six-acre park featuring statues of important state natives, shaded walkways and quiet park benches. Tours available. (Capitol Square, Mon-Fri 8-5, Sat 9-5, Sun 1-5, (919) 733-4994. Free.) [p.27, E-7]

State Legislative Building - This unique, contemporary building, completed in 1963, is devoted solely to the legislative branch of state government. Visitors are invited to watch the General Assembly proceedings when in session. (Jones St., Mon-Sat 9-5, Sun 1-5, (919) 733-7928. Free.) [p.27, E-7]

The City Market - This lively and unique complex (built in 1914) was the former city produce center and is now made up of restaurants, galleries and shops. (Martin St. at Moore.)

Attractions: Durham

CONTACT: Durham Convention and Visitors Bureau, 101 Morgan St., Durham, NC 27701 (800) 772-BULL.

Duke University - The two campuses, East and West, occupy over 8,00-acres. East Campus was originally Trinity College but West Campus is what really draws the visitors. [p.26, C-4] It's attractions include:

Duke Chapel - Great Gothic style building, reminiscent of Canterbury Cathedral in England. Don't miss the 210-foot tower with its carillon of 50 bells, (919) 684-2572. [p.26, C-4]

Duke Homestead Historic Site - The home of tobacco king Washington Duke includes the Tobacco Museum tracing the crop's history from Indian times through today. At the homestead you can also visit Duke's original tobacco factory building and farm. (Duke Historic Homestead Rd., 1/2 mile north of Jct. I-85, Guess Rd., (919) 477-5498, call for times. Free.) [p.27, B-5]

Duke Medical Center - This world renowned teaching and research facility treats over 500,00 patients annually. [p.26, C-4]

Sarah P. Duke Gardens - These 55 acres feature landscaped gardens, a lily pond, pine forest, formal terrace and rose gardens and a magnificent display of constantly changing flowers.

Main entrance on Anderson St., (919) 684-3698. [p.26, C-4]

Attractions: Chapel Hill

CONTACT: Chapel Hill - Carrboro Chamber of Commerce, 104 S Estes Dr., P.O. Box 2897, Chapel Hill, NC 27515, (919) 967-7075.

University of North Carolina at Chapel Hill was founded in 1793 and was the first state university in the country. The 3,900-acre campus has over 200 buildings. Guided tours of some of the best sights on campus, including The Old Well, Memorial Hall, Coker Arboretum and Morehead-Patterson Bell Tower are available. (For further information contact: University News Bureau, CB6210, 210 Pitsboro St., (919) 962-1630 [p.26,D-3]

GREENSBORO

Greensboro [see map p.29] was founded in 1808 and was named for the patriot, Nathaniel Greene. General Nathaniel Greene and his troops united against General Cornwallis and his men in 1781 in a wooded area in Guilford County. Though the battle was technically a defeat for the Americans, historians regard it as a pivitol battle in the Revolutionary War since the British forces were weakened considerably by Greene's army and eventually surrendered at Yorktown.

Greensboro's growth was slow at first but the arrival of the railroad in the late 1800s cemented the future of the textile industry and educational institutions that were just beginning to take root. Today Greensboro is recognized as an industrial, manufacturing and distribution center best known for the production of textiles, cigarettes and electronics.

CONTACT: Greensboro Area Convention and Visitors Bureau, 317 South Greene, Greensboro, NC 27401, (919) 274-2282.

Attractions:

Blandwood Mansion and Carriage House - The home of 19th century Governor John Motley Morehead is the oldest existing example of Tuscan Villa architecture in America. Recently restored, it appears on the National Register of Historic Places and is a National Historic Landmark (447 W. Washington St., Tue-Sat 11-2, Sun 2-5, (919) 272-5003. Admission.) [p.29, B-6]

Colonial Heritage Center and Hoskins House at Tannenbaum Park - Explore an 8-acre Revolutionary War park on the site of this former British encampment. The restored 1778 Hoskins House includes an intact kitchen, blacksmith's shed and barn. Drop by the Visitor's Center where you can view a collection of authentic era maps and browse through displays of Colonial life. (New Gaden Rd and Battleground Av, call for hours, (919) 288-8259. Free.)

Greensboro Historical Museum - The lives of Greensboro natives Dolley Madison and O. Henry are explored as are other facets of Greensboro's heritage including early settlement, transportation and military history. There is also a recreation of the historic 1960 sit-in at Woolworth's lunch counter. (130 Summit Ave., Tue-Sat 10-5, Sun 2-5, (919) 373-2043. [p.29,B-6]

Guilford Courthouse National Military Park - This is the site of the Battle of Guilford Courthouse, a pivitol conflict during the Revolutionary War in which Lord Cornwallis won the victory that eventually led to his downfall. Features wooded areas, walking trails and memorial. (6 mile north of Greensboro off U.S. 20. Daily 8:30-5, (919) 288-1776. Free.) [p.29, A-5]

Natural Science Center - A dynamic hands-on experience, attractions include zoo with 200 animals from North and South America, petting barn, planetarium, museum and nature trails. (4301 Lawndale Dr, Mon-Sat 9-5, Sun 12:30-5, (919) 288-3769. Admission.)

WINSTON-SALEM

Moravians, a Protestant sect from Pennsylvania, settled in Salem in 1766 in search of religious freedom. Their serious work ethic combined with their staunchly disciplined lifestyle led to accomplishments in the arts, music and education. Winston was founded in 1849 as an industrial center devoted to textiles, furniture-making and tobacco.

The sister cities [see map p.28] coexisted peacefully until they were incorporated into a single city in 1913. The ethnic diversity and differing backgrounds of the two towns complemented each other well. Winston-Salem, once a tobacco capital, is home to the Hanes Group, Stroh Brewing company and Westinghouse Electric Corporation. Add to this the large banking network, and you get the merger of the two cities.

CONTACT; Winston-Salem Convention and Visitor's Bureau, Chamber of Commerce, P.O. Box 1408, Winston-Salem, NC 27102, (919) 725-2361.

Attractions:

Old Salem - This was an original settlement of the Moravians from Pennsylvania in the mid 1700s. The Moravians brought old world artisan skills and were well-educated in music and language. Their 18th-century homes have been restored and the past lives again in the Old Salem business district that is open to the public. (Old Salem Road, tours daily, (919) 721-7300 for information on tours and special events.) [p.28, B-2]

Reynolda House, Museum of American Art - American paintings, artifacts, costumes and period furnishings. Formal gardens and natural woodlands are attached to the 1914 estate of the late R.J. Reynolda of the tobacco fortune. (Off Reynolda Rd. between Coliseum Dr. and Silas Creek Parkway, (919) 725-5325.) [p.28 B-2]

SciWorks - Creative hands-on exhibits delving into the worlds of natural science, physics and technology. Special exhibits on the human body, space exploration, the planet and endangered species. A 15-acre Environmental park with indigenous North Carolina habitats and 120-seat Planetarium. (400 Hanes Mill Road, Mon-Sat 10-5, Sun 1-5, (919) 767-6730. Admission.) [p.28, A-2]

The GREAT OUTDOORS

Northorth Carolina has set aside a vast amount of land as state and national parks. A description of the national parks appears in a later section [see p.62], but here is a listing by region of North Carolina's best state parks.

Whenever possible, mailing addresses and telephone numbers of the parks have been provided. Park offices are only staffed in the morning so if you need specific information on any park call the North Carolina Division of Parks and Recreation, P.O. Box 27687, Raleigh, NC 27611, (919) 733-4181.

Park hours are as follows: Nov.-Feb. 8am-6pm; March-Oct. 8am-7pm; April, May, Sept. 8am-8pm; June-Aug 8am-9pm. Nominal fees are charged by the state park system for use of camping facilities, boathouses, picnic shelter and boat rentals. Please note that fees are subject to change without notice.

The High Country

Chimney Rock Park
P. O. Box 39
Highway 64/74
Chimney Rock, NC 28720
(704) 625-9611
This park is a treat for hikers and mountain climbers. But if you don't feel like climbing, take the elevator to the summit or drive the scenic motor road. Trails lead to spectacular Hickory Nut Falls, one of the highest in the Eastern United States at 404 feet. The 27-mile long Lake Lure offers swimming, fishing and boating opportunities. Picnicking and municipal golf course. [p.5, D-6]

Lake James State Park
P. O. Box 340
Nebo, NC 28761
(704) 652-5047
Nature trails, fishing, boating, picnicking, tent camping, swimming available on 585 acres. [p.5, C-7]

Mount Jefferson State Park
P. O. Box 48
Jefferson, NC 28640
(919) 246-9653
500 acres of relatively undeveloped land with an excellent view of the Blue Ridge Mountains. Picnicking, hiking and nature study. [p.5, A-8]

Mount Mitchell State Park
Rt 5, Box 700
Burnsville, NC 28714
(704) 675-4611
Mount Mitchell, at 6,684 feet, is the highest peak east of the Mississippi. The 1,677 acre park features picnicking, hiking, nature study and some camp-ing. Seasonal restaurant and observation tower. [p.5, C-6]

New River State Park
P. O. Box 48
Jefferson, NC
(919) 982-2587
1,089-acre park features canoe-ing, primitive camping (must canoe in or walk in to camp site), hiking, fishing and nature study at four specific sites along the winding New River. The river, recognized as the second oldest in the world is noted for fantastic scenery and fishing. [p.5, A-8]

Stone Mountain State Park
Star Rt 1, Box 17
Roaring Gap, NC 28668
(919) 957-8185
13,411 acres with a granite mountain that is 600 feet high and three miles in circumfer-ence at the base. This park is especially popular with fisher-men since there are 17 miles of designated trout streams. Mountain climbing, fishing, picnicking, primitive camping and hiking. [p.6, A-2]

The Piedmont Plateau

Cliffs of the Neuse State Park
Rt 2, Box 50
Seven Springs, NC 28578
(919) 778-6234
751 acres on the Neuse River include 35 tent and trailer camp-sites as well as rowboat rentals, museum and nature center. Picnicking, fishing, swimming and hiking. [p.8, D-2]

Duke Power State Park
Rt 2, Box 224 M
Troutman, NC 28166
(704) 528-6350
1,400 acres on Lake Norman

provide swimming, fishing, boating (ramp and rentals), tent camping, trailer camping (no hookups), hiking and nature study. Organized group camping avaliable. [p.6, C-2]

Eno River State Park
6101 Cole Mill Road
Durham, NC 27705
(919) 383-1686
Most of this 2,000-acre park is undeveloped, unspoiled forest with the Eno River meandering through. Special features include a suspension bridge and a primitive camping site unreachable by automobile. Picnicking, fishing, hiking and canoeing launch site. [p.6, C-2]

Falls Lake State Rec. Area
13304 Creedmoor Rd.
Wake Forest, NC 27507
(919) 676-1027
Large lake with over 250 miles of shoreline. Boating, fishing, swimming, picnicking and camping. [p.27, B-6]

Hanging Rock State Park
Box 186
Danbury, NC 27016
(919) 593-8480
6,192 acres offering cabins and trailer sites (reservations required). Swimming, fishing, boat rentals, hiking trails, picnicking and nature study. [p.6, A-4]

Kerr Reservoir State Recreation Area
Rt 3, Box 800
Henderson, NC 27536
(919) 438-7791
800-mile shoreline on Kerr Reservoir offers picnicking,

camping, boating, swimming, fishing, waterskiing and hiking. Total project area is 106,860 acres. [p.8, A-1]

Morrow Mountain State Pk
49104 Morrow Mountain Rd
Albermarle, NC 28001
(704) 982-4402
4,693 forested, hilly acres bordered on two sides by Like Tillery,and Mountain Creek. Tent/trailer sites (no hookups), natural history museum, pool, fishing, boating (rentals and launch), hiking, riding and nature trails. Family cabins are available March-November and require advanced reservations. [p.6, D-4]

Pilot Mountain State Park
Rt 1, Box 21
Pinnacle, NC 27043
(919) 325-2355
The main attraction here is a 1,500 foot high knob-like rock formation with foor trails and a surface road to the top. Relatively undeveloped area offers picnicking and camping as well as canoeing and rafting on the Yadkin River. [p.6, A-3]

Weymouth Woods Sandhills Nature Preserve
400 North Fort Bragg Road
Southern Pines, NVC 28387
(919) 692-2167
This park offers 676 acres of sandhill natural preserve. Museum and hiking trails. [p.7, D-6]

The Coastal Plains

Carolina Beach State Pk
P. O. Box 475
Carolina Beach, NC 28428
(919)458-8206

Naturalist trail features the rare Venus Fly Trap as well as five other species of insect-eating plants. The 420 acres of the park include tent and trailer sites, picnicking, fishing, boating (ramp, marina), hiking and nature study program. [p.14, C-2]

Goose Creek State Park
Rt 2, Box 372
Washington, NC 27889
(919) 923-2191
If you're interested in waterfowl or just enjoy water-oriented activities, you'll enjoy this 1,597-acre park along the Pamlico River. Natural beaches are perfect for fishing, bird watching, swimming and boating. Hiking trails and primitive tent camping. [p.9, C-5]

Jockey's Ridge State Park
P. O. Box 592
Nag's Head, NC 27959
(919) 441-7132
This small park contains the largest natural sand dune on the East Coast. Favorite spot for hang gliders. Picnicking. [p.9, B-8]

Jones Lake State Park
Rt 2, Box 945
Elizabethtown,NC 28337
(919) 588-4550
This 2,208-acre park has 20 tent/trailer campsites as well as opportunities for picnicking, hiking, swimming, fishing and boating (rentals). [p.13, B-8]

Lake Mattamuskeet Refuge
Rt 1, Box N-2
Swan Quarter, NC 27885
(919) 926-4021

Located approximately 70 miles northeast of Washington. Administered by the U.S. Fish and Wildlife Refuge encompasses 50,000 acres of water and marshland and is a very popular spot for wintering waterfowl. [p.9, C-6]

Lake Waccamaw State Pk
Rt 1, Box 147
Lake Waccamaw, NC 28450
(919) 646-4748
Lake Waccamaw is typical of "bay" lakes found near the coast. Surrounded by cypress and swamp, it is one of the south's largest lakes. Fishing, swimming and boating. [p.14, C-1]

Merchant Millpond State Pk
Rt 1, Box 141 A
Gatesville, NC 27938
(919) 357-1191
This 2,918-acre area is dominated by a cypress swamp and huge gum tress. Large 2 1/2 mile pond offers fishing and canoeing. Picnicking, trails, camping,and primitive camping. [p.9, A-5]

Theodore Roosevelt Natural Area
P. O. Box 127
Atlantic Beach, NC 28512
(919) 726-3775
No recreation facilities are available on this unspoiled 265-acre natural area. However, nature lovers will be impressed with the rare coastal flora, nature study trail and North Carolina Aquarium. [p.15, B-5]

Skiing
North Carolina

As a southern state, North Carolina is not often thought of as a skiing mecca. However, the generous helping of mountains in the northwest region provide high elevations and climate conditions conductive to snowmaking. Combine that with breathtaking scenery, nine well-maintained ski areas and a variety of learn-to-ski programs and suddenly North Carolina is a dream for skiers of all ablilities. Below is a complete list of ski areas in North Carolina and their facilities. All areas feature snowmaking, rentals, instruction for adults and children, group rates and food concessions.

Skiing Resort	Details		Remarks
Appalachian Ski Mountain *P. O. Box 106 [p,5, B-7]* *Blowing Rock, NC 28605* *(704) 295-7828 (report)* *(800) 322-2373 (reservations)*	Vertical Drop: Slopes: Lifts:	365ft 8 3 Chair 3 Surface	Well-known for its excellence in insruction, Appalachian was the first mountain in North Carolina to install a quad chair-lift. Other features include nearby lodging and night skiing.
Cataloochee Ski Area *Rt 1, Box 502 [p.4, C-4]* *Maggie Valley, NC 28751* *(704) 926-3588 (report)* *(800) 768-0285*	Vertical Drop: Slopes: Lifts:	740ft 9 1 Chair 2 Surface	Located in the Smoky Mountains and only 40 minutes from Asheville, Cataloochee was North Carolina's first ski area. Other features include nearby lodging, cocktail lounge and night skiing.
Fairfield Sapphire Valley *4000 Highway 64* *Sapphire, NC 28774 [p.4, D-4]* *(704) 743-3441* *(800) 533- 8268 (reservations)*	Vertical Drop: Slopes: Lifts:	425 ft 4 1 Chair 1 Surface	Additional features include lodging, nightskiing and a calendar of off-season activities.
Hound Ears Lodge and Club *P.O. Box 188 [p.5, B-7]* *Blowing Rock, NC 28605* *(704) 963-4321*	Vertical Drop: Slopes: Lifts:	107 ft 2 1 Chair 1 Surface	Ideal mountain for beginners of all ages. Group and private lessons available. Lodging, off-season activities.
Ski Beech Vertical *P.O. Box 1118 [p.5, B-7]* *Banner Elk, NC 28604* *(704) 687-2011* *(800) 438-2093*	Drop: Slopes: Lifts:	830 ft 15 7 2	This resort is set high in the mountains and is home to the Southeast's only detatchable, quad chairlift. Other Chair features include: ice rink, entertainment, lodging, Surface cocktail lounge, nursery, night skiing and off-season activities.
Hawksnest Golf and Ski Resort *Town of Seven Devils [p.5, B-7]* *1800 Skyland Drive* *Banner Elk, NC 28604* *(704) 963-6563* *(800) 822-HAWK*	Vertical Drop: Slopes: Lifts:	619 ft 7 2 Chair 2 Surface	Limited ticket sales guarantee uncrowded trails. Additional features nclude nearby lodging, private lounge and night skiing.
Ski Scaly Mountain Vertical *Box 339 [p.4, D-3]* *Scaly Mountain, NC 28775*	Drop: Slopes: Lifts:	225 ft 4 1 Chair 1 Surface	Southernmost developed ski area in North Carolina P.O. offers all the amenities including lodging and night skiing.
Sugar Mountain Resort *P.O. Box 369 [p.5, B-7]* *Banner Elk, NC 28604* *(704) 898-4521* *(704) 898-5256 (report)*	Vertical Drop: Slopes: Lifts:	1,200 ft 18 5 Chair 3 Surface	Sugar Mountain has the two longest chairlifts in North Carolina. Additional features include lodging, nursery and night skiing.
Wolf Laurel Ski Slope *[p.5, B-5]* *Rt 3, Mars Hill, NC 28754* *(704) 689-4111*	Vertical Drop: Slopes: Lifts:	700 ft 15 2 Chair 1 Surface	This area offers a quad lift and challenging trails. Other features include lodging, nursery, night skiing, night skiing, iceskating, special slope for snowboarding, and off-season activities.

Annual FAIRS & FESTIVALS

JANUARY

Shooting in the New Year - Century-old German tradition in which hundreds gather as gun carriers fire blackpowder muskets into the air,chanting blessings for the New Year to be bestowed upon the town. **Cherryville** midnight, Dec. 31 through midnight Jan. 1, call (704) 435-3451.

FEBRUARY

Arts and Crafts Conference - With over 80 exhibitors, this is the largest conference in the world dedicated to antiques from the American Arts and Crafts era (1900-1915). Collectors from around the country flock to **Asheville** in mid-February to view (and purchase) these fine examples of americana. Call (704) 252-2711, ext. 8005 for more information.

MARCH

Annual Star Fiddlers Convention - For over 60 years this event has attracted fiddlers from all over the South for a Bluegrass music extravaganza. **Biscoe,** first weekend in March, call (919) 428-2972.

Spring Festival - Ski Bonanza features downhill ski racing and other snow and ski related competitions and festivities. **Seven Devils,** Hawksnest Golf and Ski Resort, first week-end in March, call (704) 963-6561.

APRIL

Annual Nature Art Show - Original art by members of the North Carolina Nature Artists Association are exhibited at SciWorks in **Winston-Salem,** generally held mid-April, call (919) 481-2187 for information.

Festival of Flowers - Profusion of flowers inside Biltmore House and in gardens and a variety of activities celebrate spring, music and dance groups, carriage parade. Biltmore Estate, **Asheville,** late April through early May, (800) 543-2961.

MAY

Alamance Balloon Fest - Outdoor festival features many events including hot air balloon races, parachuting and an airshow. **Burlington,** mid-May, call (800) 637-3804 for information.

Coca-Cola 600 - Nation's longest stock car race and part of the Winston Cup series. Charlotte Motor Speedway, **Charlotte,** Memorial Day weekend, (704) 455-3209.

Gliding Spectacular - The large sand dunes and strong offshore breezes have made the Outer Banks a very popular place to hang glide. This competition encourages participation from novices through advanced. **Nag's Head,** first weekend in May, call (800) 334-4777 for information.

Paine Webber Invitational - Senior PGA tour event attracts some of the greatest names in the game. **Piper Glen,** second weekend in May, call (704) 846-4699 for information.

RiverSpree - Dances, a parade, roadraces, food and crafts are just background to the main water events in this freshwater harbor. Continuous live entertainment performed in the park. **Elizabeth City,** Fri-Sun of Memorial Day Weekend, call (919) 335-4365 for information.

JUNE

Big Rock Blue Marlin Tournament - Week-long fishing tourney resulting in an awards banquet. Cash prizes awarded, registration required. **Morehead City,** second full week in June, call (919) 247-3575 for information.

Bud Light/American Lung Association Triathlon - 1.5K swim in Mountain Island Lake, 40K bike ride through North Mecklenburg County and a 10K run make up the largest triathlon in North Carolina. **Charlotte,** second weekend in June, call (704) 336-2584 for information.

Eastern Music Festival - Professional concert series including orchestras, chamber ensembles, recitals, Native American music performances, and special events. Guilford College, **Greensboro,** late June through July, (919) 333-7450.

"Horn In The West" - Outdoor drama performed in the town that bears his name traces the story of Daniel Boone's pioneer life. **Boone,** Daniel Boone Theater, Tue-Sun evenings late June through mid-Aug, call (704) 264-2120 for directions.

"The Lost Colony" - Pulitzer prize winning playwright Paul Green's drama about the mysterious disappearance of the first English Colony in the New World. The entire settlement, including Virginia Dare, the first child of English parents born in America, vanished without a trace sometime between 1587 and 1590.

Manteo, Mon-Sat evenings, mid-June through the end of August, call (919) 473-3414 for information.

Old Homes Tour - Tour some of the older homes and buildings in this colonial seaport town. **Beaufort,** last Fri and Sat in June, call Beaufort Historical Association, (919) 728-5225 for information.

Rogallo Kite Festival - Almost anything that can be done with a kite takes place at this annual event. Competitions, performances, instruction and demostrations. **Nag's Head,** early June, call (919) 441-4124 for information.

Singing on the Mountain - Grandfather Mountain is the setting for an all day program of old-time gospel music and preaching featuring performers from all over the country and internationally acclaimed speakers. **Linville,** Grandfather Mountain, fourth Sunday in June, call (704) 733-2013.

"Unto These Hills" - Outdoor drama depicts the history of the Cherokee· Nation from 1540 to 1838 in a natural amphitheater near the Great Smoky Mountains National Park. **Cherokee,** Mountainside Theater, Mon-Sat evenings, mid-June through late August, call (704) 497-2111 for information.

JULY

Gas Boat Drag Championships - One of the six World Championship Drag Races are held on Hollow Lake late July. **High Point,** call (919) 884-5255 for information.

Grandfather Mountain Highland Games - Gathering of over 100 Scottish clans from all over North America for track and field events as well as highland dancing and music. **Linville,** Grandfather Mountain, second full weekend in July, call (704) 733-2013 for information.

Folkmoot,USA - Representatives of many countries demonstrate their native dance, music, food and crafts. **Maggie Valley,**

11 days in late July through early August, call (704) 452-2997 for information.

AUGUST

Mountain Dance and Folk Festival - A lively event featuring cloggers, fiddlers and banjo players from all over the state. Everyone's invited to square dance–they'll teach you if you don't know how. **Asheville,** Asheville Civic Center, first week in

August, call (704) 258-3858 for information.

SEPTEMBER

Centerfest - Arists and craftsmen from all over the state display their wares in a two-day event. 250 exhibitors and continuous live entertainment. **Durham,** mid-September, call (919) 560-2787 for information.

Durham Blues Festival - A weekend full of R&B, zydeco, contemporary and traditional blues performed by national and local talent. **Durham,** Athletic Park, last weekend in September, call (919) 560-2787 for information.

North Carolina Apple Festival - Area locations feature crafts, food, entertainment, Apple parade, mountain dance jamboree, gospel concert, antique car show, antique airplane fly-by, Gem & Mineral Spectacular, and street dance with a Shagging night. **Hendersonville,** Labor Day weekend, call (800) 828-4244.

OCTOBER

Chrysanthemum Festival - Street festival and Octoberfest includes arts crafts and tours through Tryon Place Historic Sites and Gardens in celebration of the blooming chrysanthemums. **New Bern,** early October, (919) 638-5781.

Piedmont Crafts Fair - Huge display of Southeastern U.S. arts and crafts are for sale. **Winston-Salem,** Benton Convention Center, third weekend in October, call (919) 725-1516 for information.

Randolph County Fall Festival - Outdoor festival featuring handmade crafts, native food and plenty of country and bluegrass music. **Asheville,** first weekend in October, call (919) 626-2626 for information.

NOVEMBER

Handel's Messiah - The Christmas Season begins with the traditional performance of the holiday classic in the magnificent Duke Chapel. First weekend in December. **Durham,** Duke University Chapel, call (919) 684-3898 for information.

DECEMBER

An Eastern European Christmas - Annual family festival featuring live music, crafts and food from Eastern Europe. **Raleigh,** North Carolina Museum of Art, first weekend in December, call (919) 833-1935 for information.

A BRIEF HISTORY OF

SOUTH CAROLINA

South Carolina's turbulent history spans over 400 years and is firmly interwoven with the fabric of the American experience. South Carolina, as one of the first settlements in the New World, distinguished itself as a worthy opponent in the American Revolution. The state was also the originator of secession, the birthplace of the Civil War, and ultimately a survivor in the South's struggle for social and economic strength in modern times.

Before the first permanent settlement at Charles Town, two earlier attempts at colonization were thwarted. An attempt by the Spanish to establish a settlement in 1562 near present day Georgetown was foiled by an especially harsh winter and Indian attack, while an attempt by French Huguenots, led by Jean Ribaut in 156, was abandoned a short time later. Finally, in 1670 King Charles of England magnanimously gave the Carolinas to eight noblemen. The Lords Proprietors settled at Albemarle Point where they remain for 10 years before moving to what is now Charleston.

By the mid-1700s new townships were developed inland and the Welsh, Scottish and Germans who had settled upcountry in the Piedmont Plateau had a less lofty lifestyle than their aristocratic English counterparts along the coastal plains. This caused stress between the two factions since everyone paid taxes but the landed aristocracy in the low country was better represented and virtually controlled the government. At about this time, the Indian population was decreasing as a result of diseases brought by European settlers and

forced relocation westward. As the Indians were forced out, blacks were brought in from Africa and the West Indies and it wasn't long before slaves on rice and indigo plantations outnumbered the white population by two to one.

South Carolina took an active role in the Revolutionary War. 137 battles and skirmishes took place on South Carolina soil, more than any other colony. Several battles figure prominently in the progress of the Revolution: The Battle of Fort Moultrie was the first decisive victory for the Americans while the hour-long Battle of Kings Mountain on October 7, 1780 stopped Cornwallis' move into North Carolina giving the Americans time to prepare and strategize. In 1786 the capital was moved from Charleston to Columbia, thus easing strained relations between upcountry farmers and low country plantation owners. On May 23, 1788, South Carolina became the eighth state to ratify the Constitution and join the Union.

After the Revolution, business thrived in South Carolina. Fortunes were made by harvesting cotton and indigo on large platations. Rice was also a lucrative crop. Brought over from Africa, it required hours of back-breaking work in its harvesting but the widespread use of slaves along with the increased importation of them between 1790 and 1808 made planters even more wealthy. The future looked bright for South Carolina's landed aristocracy. The invention of the cotten gin guaranteed larger production, volume and ultimately more money. But slavery, upon which plantation owners so heavily depended, was beginning to divide the country.

On December 20, 1860 the Ordinance of Secession was signed in Charleston and South Carolina became the first state to secede from the Union. Fort Sumter, where the first shots of the Civil War rang out, fell in April of 1861. Though few battles of this war were fought on South Carolina soil, the state was hit hard during the War Between the States. Over one-fifth of the state's white males were killed, most of the coastal areas fell into Union hands and General William T. Sherman left a trail of smoldering ruins behind him as he worked his way north from Savannah, Georgia.

South Carolina struggled with social, political and economic turmoil for years after Reconstruction. It took almost until World War II to build a strong economy based on industry and agriculture. The textile industry in particular provided the backbone of the economy which still survives today. Textiles, which were originally a New England craft, spread to and grew in South Carolina due to low transportation costs for cotton and cheap Southern labor costs. This favorable business environment attracted establishment northern textile companies and provided incentive for them to move south. Tourism is now the second largest industry in the state, followed by agribusiness. Peaches, cotton, tobacco and livestock are among the state's largest commodities.

Today South Carolina attracts visitors and new residents from all over the country. Its pleasing climate and beautiful terrain, combined with the abundance of outdoor and recreational opportunities make it thoroughly inviting place to live or visit.

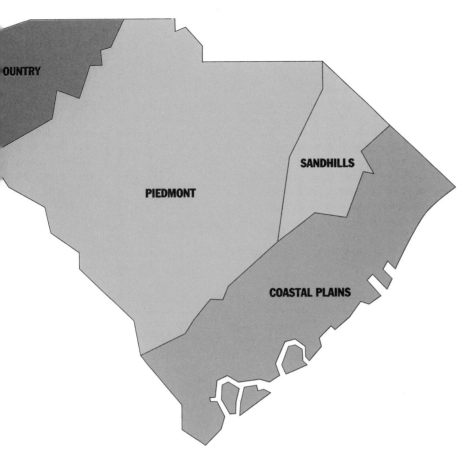

OUNTRY

PIEDMONT

SANDHILLS

COASTAL PLAINS

Exploring the Regions of South Carolina

The best way to understand South Carolina is by region. Although not a large state–in fact it's the south's smallest–South Carolina is very diverse. Not like North Carolina, the rugged mountains of South Carolina give away to a large Piedmont region, then to a sandy strip known as the Sandhills, and finally to the expansive Coastal plain. The contrast in topography offers an abundance of recreational opportunities and spectacular sightseeing.

Upcountry South Carolina

The Blue Ridge Region of South Carolina, commonly known as Upcountry South Carolina, is located in the upper northwest corner of the state. Here, rivers rush

through granite passes, and round-topped mountains rise to heights of over 3,000 feet. You can hike through oak and hickory woodlands or camp under the stars in a vast pine forest. Dry, rocky terrain gives way to apple and peach orchards ripe for the picking. Along with beauty, there's history in these hills. The Cherokee Foothills Scenic Highway [p.10, A-4] which extends south from the North Carolina border to the Georgia border is picturesque as well as historic. Along this route you'll find well-maintained state parks and National Historical Sites dating back to the Revolutionary War. Whether you decide to go whitewater rafting or take a leisurely drive, you're sure to be impressed with all that Upcountry Carolina has to offer.

Attractions

Chattooga National Wild and Scenic River is flanked by the Sumter National Forest. Scenes from the film "Deliverance" were shot on location here. The river begins in the Blue Ridge mountains in North Carolina and serves as the state line between South Carolina and Georgia for

over 40 miles. It is a whitewater rafter's and kayaker's delight with rapids occasionally interrupted by calm, still pools. Information on tours can be obtained by the National Forest Service in Columbia at (803) 765-5222. [p.10, A-3].

Clemson Univerity in Clemson is a grand institution that was founded in 1889. Over 17,000 students study at the campus which is well-known for its football team. The University Visitors Center will lead you in a guided tour if you wish. Don't miss the 208-acre South Carolina Botanical Gardens with over 2,200 varieties of plants and flowers. (803) 656-4789. [p.10, B-4]

Cowpens National Battlefield near Chesnee was the scene of the American Patriots' most decisive victory over the British on January 17, 1781. During the battle, American casualties were minimal while the Red Coats lost over 100 men with many more wounded. Cornwallis, with his troops considerable weakened, surrendered at Yorktown the following October. (803) 461-2828. [p.11, A-7]

Pendelton Historical and Recreational District headquartered in Pendelton actually encompasses a three country area including Anderson, Oconee and Pickens. The area was settled in the late 1700s and is formerly Indian Territory. Key attractions include Pendelton Farmers Society Hall, Hunter's Store and several historical homes. (803) 646-3782. [p.11, B-5]

The Piedmont

The Piedmont Region of South Carolina is similar to the Piedmont in North Carolina. It occupies a large central segment of the state, with rolling hills, and deep valleys interspersed with fertile farmland. Throughout the spring, the region is colored with blooming plants and flowering trees. This area is also known as South Carolina's Freshwater Coast with picturesque lakes and meandering rivers cutting through the sometimes rocky terrain. Much of the Piedmont was once occupied by the British during the Revolutionary War and as such is historically significant.

Attractions

Abbeville, a charming, historical town, is known as the "Birthplace of the Confederacy" since it was here that the original secession document was presented. Established in 1758, it is also the birthplace of one of South Carolina's most famous sons, John C. Calhoun. Be sure to stop by the beautifully restored Opera House. (803) 459-4600. [p.11, C-5]

Ninety-Six National Historical Site in Ninety-Six is operated by the National Park Service. Originally a frontier settlement, the site has an extensive history. Battles of the French and Indian War and the first battle of the American Revolution waged on South Carolina soil was fought here. Structures and ruins from both of these time periods can be seen and archaeological excavations are uncovering 18th and 19th century artifacts. (803) 984-2233. [p.11, C-6]

Paramount's Carowinds, 10 miles south of Charlotte, NC, is the nation's only amusement park in two states. The 83-acre park straddles the North and South Carolina border and features rides, games, entertainment and water oriented amusements. (803) 548-5300, (800) 888-4FUN. [p.12, A-2]

Pottersville Museum in Edgefield recounts the history of pottery and its vital role as a once-major industry in the area. The museum also contains a rare potter collection from the 18th and 19th centuries. (803) 637-3333. [p.11, D-7]

Springdale Course in Camden is host to some of the country's richest and most prestigious steeplechase races. " The Colonial Cup" and the " Carolina Cup" take place here each spring. (803) 432-6513. [p.1, C-3]

Union County Museum in Union contains an impressive collection of Civil War artifacts and Civil War era tools, equipment and memorabilia. (803) 427-9039. [p.11, B-7]

Note: See listings under Columbia for more Piedmont region attractions.

The Sandhills

The Sandhills region of the state is a very narrow area wedged between the Piedmont and the upper Coastal Plains. It is distinction from the rest of the state is largely topographical. The Sandhills were formed from ancient dunes when millions of years ago the sea extended to the middle of the state. Streams coming from the rocky terrain of the Piedmont terminate abruptly as they reach the soft, loose infertile soil of the Sandhills region.

Attractions

Carolina Sandhills Wildlife Refuge just four miles north of McBee is 45,586 acres of the unusual sandhill terrain. Many species of wildlife live here including the nation's

sixth largest population of the red-cockaded woodpecker. Facilities at the refuge include hiking trails, picnicking, observation decks. (803) 335-8401. [p.12, B-4]

Chesterfield is unique in that it lies almost entirely in the Sandhills Region. The seat of Chesterfeild County, the town has 1500 residents and was established in 1798. (803) 623-2343. [p.12, B-4]

The Coastal Plains

The Coastal Plains of South Carolina extend from the shores north of Myrtle Beach down to the southernmost resort islands and inland to the Sandhills. The murky swampland and lush marshes give way to the beaches, bays and barrier islands of the coast. A geologist would argue that the Coastal Plains of South Carolina stretch even further since the con-

tinental shelf extends for over 60 miles from shore underneath the Atlantic Ocean. **Historic Charleston** is located along the Coastal Plains as is the famous Grand Strand (see p. 23). These areas are South Carolina's most popular vacation spots. Visitors from all over the country as well as South Carolinians themselves flock to these famous beaches year-round. Here you'll find every type of water sport available. Readers of Pat Conroy novels, such as The Prince of Tides will recognize the rich lowlands and nurturing marshland of the state.

Attractions

Cheraw State Fish Hatchery in Cheraw is a breeding area for large and small mouth bass, channel catfish and other fish indigenous to the area. Features a picnic area and aquarium. (803) 537-7628. [p.13, B-5]

Georgetown is a historic seaport which has recently deepened its channel and is beginning to build up its shipping traffic again.

Founded in 1729, Georgetown was a major export center prior to the Civil War and was instrumental in shipping rice, indigo and cotton from prosperous plantations to England. There's much to see here including the Rice Museum, Brookgreen Gardens, Hopsewee Plantation and the Harold Kaminski House. (800) 777-7705. [p.17, A-8]

Kiawah Island is a truly special place to visit. Not far from Beaufort or Charleston, it's a rich, well-preserved and protected environment reachable only by a wooded bridge over the Kiawah River. It is home to a multitude of deer, racoon and alligator as well as the endangered loggerhead sea turtle that tips the scale at over 400 pounds. There are two resorts on the island but most of it has been preserved for environmental and wildlife study. Much of the island is untouched and remains the same as it was when Indians hunted and fished

here. (803) 768-2121 [p.17, C-6]

Penn School Historic District and Museum on St. Helena Island is also historically important to South Carolina and the Low Country. During the Civil War the Penn School was established as the first school for freed slaves in the South. The York W. Bailey Museum illustrates the culture and heritage of 18th and 19th century blacks along the sea islands. (803) 838-2235. [p.17, C-5]

Port Royal is one of South Carolina's earliest port towns. The quiet community retains much of the atmosphere of its fishing village past and its views from the boardwalk and observation towers are magnificent. (803) 524-3163. [p.16, C-4]

Walterboro was once a summer resort for wealthy plantation owners. There is some significant 19th century architecture here. Don't miss the Colleton Museum with exhibits pertaining to the culture and history of Colleton County. (803) 549-9595.

CITY LIGHTS

IN SOUTH CAROLINA

*The cities of South Carolina are as diverse
as the state itself–you'll find natural wonders and
historic landmarks, prestigious institutions of
higher learning hosting modern cultural exhibits,
and old-time manufacturing plants next to
technological research and development labs.
And wherever you go
you're sure to find the hospitality of which
South Carolinians are so proud.*

COLUMBIA

Columbia [see map p.21] was established as the capital of South Carolina in 1786 because of its proximity to the geographic center of the state. The city, on the site of an old plantation, was a compromise between wealthy Charlestonian planters and upcountry farmers who each wanted to be close to the state capital and fairly represented in the state legislature. The city is noted for its advanced design and tumultuous history. The broad avenues, (over 150 feet wide), are laid out in a checkerboard design because the common wisdom dictated that stagnant air and close quarters caused malaria. This planned, grid style is very unusual for a city so old.

Columbia figures prominently in the evolution of the Civil War and its aftermath. It was here on December 17, 1860 that the Ordinance of Secession was passed at the First Baptist Church. Though it was eventually signed in Charleston due to a smallpox epidemic in the capital, Union forces were especially vengeful when they attatcked Columbia. Sherman arrived on February 2, 1865 and virtually annihilated the city. Over 80 blocks and 1,400 buildings were burned so that very little of what exists in Columbia today pre-dates the Civil War. Ironically, the First Baptist Church did survive. Legend has it that Union invaders were determined to destroy the place where the Ordinance of Secession was drawn up but were purposely misled by a clever Columbian who directed them to the Methodist church instead. Locals saved Trinity Cathedral from the conflagration by hoisting a cross atop the roof and disguising it as a Catholic church. Sherman's wife, they knew, was Catholic and the church was spared.

Reconstruction was a slow, arduous process. What eventually emerged is an inviting integration of a busy capital city and a friendly college town. The legislature meets in the state house each year between January and May and the University of South Carolina Gamecocks, now members of the South Eastern Conferences delight football fans throughout the fall. The city also supports minor league baseball's Capital City Bombers as well as the oldest continuing community theater in the country. Though history has been especially rough on Columbia, it remains a charming, historic city with much to see.

CONTACT: Columbia Metropolitan Convention and Visitor's Center, 1012 Gervais St., Columbia, SC 29201, (803) 254-0479.

Attractions

Governor's Mansion - South Carolina's governors have lived here since 1868. First built as officers' quarters at a military academy, it was the only building on the grounds left standing after Sherman's conflagration. (800 Richland St., tours by appointment Tue-Thu, (803) 737-1710. Free.) [p.21, C-6]

Mann-Simons Cottage - Home of Celia Mann, a slave born in Charleston. She purchased her freedom in the early 1800s and walked to Columbia to begin a new life. Her home is now a museum of African American culture portraying the evolution of Southern Blacks. (1403 Richland St., Tue-Sat 10 am-3:15 pm, Sun 1:15-4:15. (803) 252-1450. Free)

Riverbanks Zoo - Natural habitat zoo creatively designed with minimum use of bars and cages. Features over 800 animals from around the world. (Greystone Blvd and I-126. Daily 9-5. (803) 779-8717. Admission.) [p.21, C-5]

Robert Mills Historic House and Park - Residence of South Carolina's best known architect whose work includes the Washington Monument. Built in 1823, the house is an outstanding example of the Regency period. (1616 Blanding St., Tue-Sat 10:15-3:15, Sun 1:15-4:15. (803) 252-7742. Admission.) [p.21, C-6]

South Carolina State Museum - Long before it was the State Museum, this renovated textile mill was the first in the world to be totally electric. Today its four floors are devoted to art, history, natural history, science and technology. Special features include many hands-on exhibits and a permanent laser display. Emphasis is given to South Carolina's contributions to the above mentioned subject areas. (301 Gervais St., Mon-Sat 10-5. Sun 1-5, (803) 737-4595. Admission.) [p.21, D-6]

State House - The legislature is in session from January through early June and visitors are invited to watch South Carolinians make their laws from the public galleries in both houses. The Capitol building is widely recognized as one of the most beautiful in the country. After touring the impressive interior be sure to view the six bronze stars on the exterior western wall which indicate where cannonball marks were inflicted by General Sherman's Army during the Civil War. (Main and Gervais Streets, Mon-Fri 9-5, (803) 734-2430. Free.) [p.21, D-6]

The Columbia Museum of Art - Besides a fun hands-on exhibit and the multi-media Gibbes Planetarium, the museum houses an impressive collection of Renaissance, Baroque and contemporary art. (1112 Bull St., Tue-Fri 10-5, Sat-Sun 12:30-5, (803) 799-2810. Free.) [p.21, D-6]

Trinity Cathedral - Home of the 6th largest Episcopal congregation in the country, it is the oldest church building in Columbia and a fine example of English Gothic architecture. The design of the building was copied from the York Cathedral in England. (1100 Sumter St., Call (803) 771-7300 for tour information.) [p.21, D-6]

University of South Carolina - (Bounded by Gregg, Pendelton and Main Streets, (803) 777-7700 for tour info. Free.) Many points of interest are located on this lovely, historic campus that has many times been the background for Civil War and antebellum era Hollywood films. Aside from the grounds themselves, don't miss the **Horseshoes**. It is the original campus area that dates back to the early 19th century. Its buildings are listed in the National Register of Historic Places. The area was spared during the Civil War because it was set up as a medical center that attended wounded soldiers both Union and Confederate. Also worth a visit while on campus is the **McKissick Museum,** (803) 777-5400.) Located at the head of the Horseshoe, it features revolving exhibits on art, history and the natural sciences. Of special interest is the impressive collection of 20th Century-Fox Movietone Newsreels, the Bernard M. Baruch Silver Gallery and the J. Harry Howard Gemstone Collection. (Mon-Fri 9-4, Sat 10-5, Sun 1-5. Free.) [p.21, D-6]

CHARLESTON

The mere mention of the place conjures up images of stately, aristocratic homes, charming cobblestone streets and cultivated, mannered Southerners. A visit confirms all expectations. Walking the serene narrow avenues of the city and admiring its antebellum homes, it is hard to imagine its tumultuous history of war and natural disaster.

Charleston [see map p.19] is the narrow peninsula that protrudes between the Ashley and Cooper Rivers to create a busy Atlantic port. Charles Towne, as it was once known, was the first permanent settlement in the Carolinas. Capital of South Carolina until 1786, Charleston possessed an aristocratic tradition that still exists today. Wealth and refinement in Charleston came from the prosperity enjoyed by plantation owners whose most abundant and lucrative crops included rice and indigo. By the mid-1770s, Charleston was a strategic port on the Eastern seaboard as well. Its strength, coupled with Charlestonians desire to remain independent, allowed the city to stave off British attack in 1776. In fact, a surprising amount of the city is pre-revolutionary even though it is more often considered a Civil War era city. Charleston's most dubious distiction is that it is where the Civil War began. On April 12, 1861, troops at Fort Johnson fired upon Union-held Fort Sumter, strategically located at the entrance to Charleston harbor. The two day bombardment resulted in the surrender of Fort Sumter to Confederate troops and the beginning of the War Between the States.

A visit to historic Charleston is like taking a step back in time. Despite the many fires and hurricanes (most recently Hugo) that have ravaged the city, most of it remains intact, well-maintained and downright pampered by the proud residents of the community. You'll be lulled back in time by the hypnotic clang of century-old church bells as you tour one of Charleston's magnificent estates. Or, indulge in the local speciality, She-Crab Soup, while admiring the boats in Charleston harbor. However you choose to spend your time, expect to be entertained and romanced by the allure of old Charleston.

CONTACT: Charleston Trident Convention and Visitors Bureau, P. O. Box 975, Charleston, SC 29402, (803) 853-8000.

Attractions

Cabbage Row - This row of homes got its name in the early 1800s because the black tenants who lived there would display cabbage and other vegetables for sale on the windowsills. The block was immortalized as "Catfish Row" by Du Bose Heyward in his novel, "Porgy and Bess" was based. (89-81 Church Street) [p.19, E-6]

Charleston Single Houses - You will encounter many fine examples of this unique type of residential architecture during any tour of the city. Single Houses were designed for the deep, narrow lots of the old city and to avoid the steep taxes the British levied on street front property. The doorway on the street invariably opens to a porch or piazza which leads to the formal entrance of the house in the center of the porch. In Charleston, piazzas are always located on the south or north of the house to protect it from the burning summer sun and to provide cross ventilation from southwesterly breezes. The term "single house" comes from the fact that they are only one room wide. Best examples of single houses are: Andrew Hasell House, 64 Meeting Street; Colonel Issac Motte House, 30 Meeting Street, and the "Three Sisters" at 23, 25, 17 Meeting Street.

Drayton Hall - A National Historic Landmark that was built between 1738-1742, Drayton Hall is an outstanding example of Georgian-Palladian residential architecture. Until 1969, this quintessential southern plantation was home to seven generations of the Drayton family. (9 miles northwest of Charleston on Highway 61. Call (803) 766-0188 for directions and hours. Admission.) [p.19. B-5]

Fort Sumter - The only way to get to this historic island is by boat. The Civil War began here, making the site one of the nation's most significant landmarks. The tour offers a scenic view of Charleston Harbor and a unique perspective on Charleston itself. (Tour boats depart from Patriots Point and City Marina; call Fort Sumter Tours at (803) 722-1691 for information.) [p.19, E-7]

The Battery and Charleston Harbor - (Located at the southern tip of the city.) The Battery, also known as White Point Garden, is a park that commemorates Charlestonians and the battles that they fought throughout the city's history. Of special interest are the cannons which were captured from Union forces during the Battle of Fort Sumter and used against Northern soldiers for the remainder of the Civil War. Charleston Harbor is where (Charlestonians claim) "the Ashley and Cooper Rivers meet to form the Atlantic Ocean." From here you can see Fort Sumter, Fort Johnson, James Island and Fort Moultrie. [p.19. E-6,7]

The Historic homes, churches and other buildings of Charleston are best enjoyed at a leisurely pace. Many walking and carriage ride tours are available. Pick up a copy of the "Complete Walking Tour of Historic Charleston." Put out by the Charleston Publishing Co., it offers an extremely inexpensive, enjoyable way to explore and learn all about Charleston at your own place. A copy can be secured at the Charleston Visitor Information Center, 375 Meeting St., Charleston, SC 29402

The Market - This open air stall market is busy all day and sells everything from fresh vegetables to local crafts. Of special interest are the Flower Ladies who sell vibrant bunches of flowers from the nearby islands, and the Basket Ladies who weave beautiful creations by using an old technique brought over from Africa centuries ago. (Between Meeting and East Bay Streets.) [p.19, D-6]

U.S.S. Yorktown - " The Fighting Lady" saw extensive combat during World War II. The vessel is now the country's largest maritime museum and visitors are free to explore the bridge, flight deck, mess hall, captains quarters and much more. (Patriot's Point, Mt. Pleasant side of Cooper River Bridge, 2 miles north off U.S. 17, Open daily, (803) 884-2727. Admission.) [p.19, E-7]

HILTON HEAD ISLAND

Hilton Head Island [see map p.25] was first settled in the 1700s after it had been claimed for England by Captain William Hilton in 1663. The community that developed prospered until the Civil War when it was used by the North as a watchpost and then deserted. After the war, mush of the island was parceled off and designated for ownership by freed slaves. Reconstruction virtually passed Hilton Head by and the island was allowed to atrophy until developers arrived in the 1950s.

What Hilton Head lacks in historical, commercial and industrial attributions it makes up for in its fantastic natural assets. The sneaker-shaped island anchors South Carolina's coastline. Its 42 square miles make it the largest sea island between New Jersey and Florida. Contemporary Hilton Head is largely credited to Charles Fraser, a developer who spawned remarkable growth of the island by attracting tourists and new residents while protecting the island's natural beauty. Fraser first built " Sea Pines Resort." Residential buildings in these strategically placed developments are purposely understated and are painted in natural shades so as to blend into the surrounding wooded area.

Besides Sea Pines, there is Shipyard, Wexford, Palmetto Dunes, Port Royal, Indigo Run and Hilton Head Resorts. Harbortown, located in Sea Pines is the most commercially developed area and boasts a number of shops, restaurants and galleries. Because over 1 1/2 million visitors visit Hilton Head annually, tourism is by far the largest industry. However, this planned community maintains a laid-back island lifestyle and never has an overcrowded feeling. Hilton Head offers visitors the choice to relax

for hours on the beach or pack every moment with swimming, sailing, tennis or golf. After all, the island has 28 golf courses, over 300 tennis courts, and miles and miles of coastline.

One of the joys of visiting Hilton Head Island is that there is no pressure to sight-see. There are no historic homes or important art museums–the best sights are the sand, sea, sky and fairways. Following is a list of attractions on or near Hilton Head Island.

CONTACT: Hilton Head Island Chamber of Commerce, P.O. Box 5647, Hilton Head Island, SC 29938, (803) 785-3673.

Attractions

Beaufort - For a small town (pop. 9,657) Beautfort boasts a colorful history and is loaded with significant architecture. The town, the second oldest in South Carolina, was captured by the British during the Revolutionary War and was later occupied by Union troops during the Civil War. Be sure to stop by the Historic Beautfort Foundation at 801 Bay Street for a map of the town's landmarks. (803) 524-6334. [p.16, C-4]

Daufuskie Island - Just a short boat ride from Harbor Town Marina or Shelter Cove Harbor and you've turned back the clock over 100 years. Remnants of antebellum days are scattered all over the island but the real attraction here is the undisturbed natural beauty of the environment. A century old house was painstakingly moved to the island recently and is the perfect setting for an extra special meal. (For information on excursions call (803)

785-3673.) [p.25, C-7]

Harbor Town Marina - The sailing hub of Hilton Head, the marina provides plenty of fun even if you don't own a boat. You can rent or charter one or enjoy cocktails in one of the restaurants while watching the sunset. Be sure to take note of the impressive " Liberty Oak" at the center of the marina. The original plans for Harbor Town included its demolition but instead, plans were re-worked and the tree now sits on its own peninsula, a place of honor among the eclectic collection of sea faring vessels. [p.16, D-4]

Parris Island - Ex-Marine or not, it's interesting to visit the U. S. Marine Corps Recruit Depot. It's the first stop for all Marine recruits east of the Mississippi. Guided tours are available and visitors are invited to watch formations and young recruits struggling through the famous obstacle course at Leatherneck Square. (Open to visitors 10-4:30 daily, (803) 525-2951. Free.) [p.16, D-4]

GREENVILLE & SPARTANBURG

Greenville and Spartanburg are located amid the foothills and apple orchard of Upcountry Carolina. Two of the most populated and industrialized cities in the state, each is noted for its abundance of textiles and manufacturing plants and national headquarters for many foreign companies such as BMW. Greenville has almost 700 plants producing everything from fabrics to plastics and heavy machinery while Spartanburg is one of the largest peach producers in the nation.

Attractions: Greenville

CONTACT: Greater Greenville Convention and Visitors Bureau, P.O. Box 10527, Greenville, SC 29603, (803) 233-0461.

Gallery of Sacred Art and Bible Lands Museum - One of the world's best and largest collections of sacred art and rare Biblical materials. Rembrandt and Rubens. (Located on the campus of Bob Jones University at Jct. U.S. 29, SC 291 Tue-Sat 2-5, (803) 242-5100 x1050. Free.) [p.24, E-2]

Greenville County Museum of Art - Impressive collection of Southern related paintings by Georgia O'Kaefe, Helen Turner, Jasper Johns and others. (420 College Street, Tue-Sat 10-5, Sun 1-5, (803) 271-7570. Donation.) [p.24, E-1]

Greenville Zoo - Besides finding over 200 animals,and a reptile building, visitors can picnic, play tennis, jog, hike and bike on the grounds. (E. Washington Street, Daily 10-4:30, (803) 467-4300.) [p.24. E-1]

Attractions: Spartanburg

CONTACT: Spartanburg Tourism and Convention Bureau, P.O. Box 1636, Spartanburg, SC 29304-1636, (803) 594-5050.

Spartanburg Arts Center - Changing art exhibits are displayed and classes in the visual and performing arts are offered. (385 S. Spring St., Mon-Fri 9-5, Sat 10-2, Sun 2-5, (803) 583-2776. Free.) [p.30, F-2]

Spartanburg County Regional Museum - Exhibits depict Upcountry history and memorabilia. (501 Otis Blvd. at Pine, Tue-Sat 10-12, and 3-5, Sun 2-5, (803) 596-3501. Admission.) [p.30, F-2]

Walnut Grove Plantation - Fully restored and authentically furnished girlhood home of Kate Moore Barry, a Revolutionary War heroine who was a scout for General Morgan at the Revolutionary Battle of Cowpens. The home is the center of a complete plantation featuring a school, smokehouse, barn and doctor's office. (Near Jct. U.S. 221 and I-26, Tue-Sat 11-5, April-Oct., Sundays year-round, (803) 576-6546. Admission.) [p.11, A-7]

The GREAT OUTDOORS

Below is a regional listing of selected state parks in South Carolina. For additional information on any of these parks call or write the South Carolina Division of State Parks, PRT, Edgar Brown Building, 1205 Pendelton St., Columbia, SC 29201, (803) 734-0156.

The Coastal Plains

Cape Romain National Wildlife Refuge
Near Moore's Landing, off U.S. 17 North, 20 miles north of Charleston
(803) 928-3368
The 60,000-acre refuge, made up of barrier islands and salt marshes, is one of the nation's best wildlife preserves. [p.17, B-7]

Colleton State Park
Canadys, SC 29433
(803) 538-8206
Small but pleasant shady park along the banks of the Edisto River. Camping (25 sites), nature trails, picnicking, fishing. [p.16, B-4]

Edisto Beach State Park
Edisto Island, SC 29438
(803) 869-2156
Perfect for beach lovers, this park features three miles of beach with cabins by the marsh and over 100 campsites near the ocean. Swimming, camping, fishing, hiking and picnicking. [p.17, C-5]

Givhans Ferry State Park
Ridgeville, SC 29472
(803) 873-0692
Overlooking the Edisto River, this park provides cabins and 25 campsites. Fishing, hiking, swimming and boating. [p.17, B-5]

Huntington Beach State Pk
Murrells Inlet, SC 29576
(803) 237-4440
"Atalaya," the castle-like studio and former home of famous sculptor Anna Hyatt Huntington, is located in this popular park. Boardwalk, swimming, fishing, hiking, picnicking, camping (127 sites) and hiking trails. [p.13, D-7]

Hunting Island State Park
St. Helena Island, SC 29920
(803) 838-2011
The 5,000-acres of beaches, forest and marshland were once primarily used for hunting deer and waterfowl. The 133-foot Hunting Island lighthouse provides a superb view of the island and ocean. Swimming, fishing, picnicking, nature programs, campsites, 15 vacation cabins and zoo. [p.17, D-5]

Myrtle Beach State Park
Hwy 17 S.
Myrtle Beach, SC 29577
(803) 238-5325
One of South Carolina's most popular parks. Features camping (350 sites) and cabins, ocean and pool swimming, fishing, hiking, picnicking and nature trail. [p.13, D-7]

Old Dorchester State Park
300 State Park Road
Summernille, SC 29485-8431
(803) 873-1740
This 97-acre park was settled in 1697 by Congregationalists from Massachusetts. It was abandoned in 1778 but visitors can still view the ruins of the Church of the 18th-cantury town and the walls of the old fort. Picnicking, fishing, relics and artifacts on display in interpretive building. [p.17, B-6]

The Sandhills

Little Pee Dee State Park
Rt 2, Box 250
Dillon, SC 29536
(803) 774-8872
Anglers love this park since the Little Pee Dee River is brimming with bream, a very

tasty panfish. Boating (rentals), fishing, swimming, camping (50 sites), picnicking and nature trails. [p.13, C-6]

Old Santee Canal State Pk
900 Stoney Landing Rd.
Moncks Corner, SC 29461
(803) 899-5200
The park is over a mile long and includes the historic Santee Canal which was completed in 1800 and was the first man-made channel canal in the U.S. Canoe rental, nature trails picnicking, interpretive center, Berkeley County Museum. [p.17, A-5]

Woods Bay State Park
Rt 1, Box 208
Olanta, SC 29114
(803) 659-4445
The main attraction of this 1,541-acre park is an elliptical-shaped swappy depression known as "Carolina Bay." One theory says it was formed thousands of years ago by a meteor shower or broken comet. Park also includes fantastic plant and wildlife (even alligators). Fishing, canoe rental and picnicking. [p.12, D-4]

The Piedmont

Aiken State Park
1145 State Park Road
Windsor, SC 29856
(803) 649-2857
Plenty of water-oriented activities are available at this park which includes four spring-fed lakes and the South Edisto River. Swimming, boating (rental), fishing, picnicking, camping (25 sites) and nature trails. [p.16, A-2]

Andrew Jackson State Pk
196 Andrew Jackson State Pk Rd
Lancaster, SC 29720
(803) 285-3344
The museum and one-

room schoolhouse commemorate where our seventh President, Andrew Jackson was born. Recreational activities here include fishing, boating, picnicking and camping. [p.12, A-2]

Barnwell State Park
Rt 2, Box 147
Blackville, SC 29817
(803) 284-2212
One very special feature at this 307-acre park is the Sol Blatt Recreation Center for the Handicapped. Other features include swimming, boating (rentals), fishing, picnicking, camping (25 sites) rental cabins and nature trail. [p.16, A-3]

Cheraw State Park
Hwy 52
Cheraw, SC 29520
(803) 537-2215

Large park offering camping, fishing, picnicking, swimming, boat rentals and bridal paths. Cabins for rent, call for information. [p.12, B-4]

Dreheer Island State Park
Rt 1, Box 351
Prosperity, SC 29127
(803) 364-3530
Three islands on popular Lake Murray with 12 miles of shoreline. Swimming, fishing, boating (ramps and rentals), picnicking, camping (112 campsites, some of them lakefront). [p.11, C-8]

Hickory Knob St Resort Pk
Rt 1, Box 199-B
McCormick, SC 29835
(803) 391-2450

This park has a modern 80-unit guest lodge as well as nine duplex cottages overlooking Strom Thurmond Lake, if camping is not your thing. Fishing, boat rentals, golfing, nature trails and tennis. [p.11, D-5]

Kings Mountain State Park
1277 Park Rd.
Blacksburg, SC 29702
(803) 222-3209
The focal point of this 6,141-acre park is the "Living Farm," an 18th century frontier homestead. Swimming, fishing, boating, picnicking and camping. [p.11, A-8]

Lake Greenwood State Park
302 State Park Rd.
Ninety Six, SC 29666
(803) 543-3535
Over 914-acres on Greenwood lake. Fishing, swimming, boating, waterskiing, picnicking and camping (125 sites). [p. 11, C-6]

Lake Wateree State Park
Rt 4, Box 282E5
Winnsboro, SC 29180
(803) 482-6126
Near Columbia, this 238-acre park offers camping (72 sites), picnicking and boating. [p.12, B-2]

Upcountry South Carolina

Ceasar's Head State Park
8155 Geer Hwy
Cleveland, SC 29635
(803) 836-6115
This park is named for the side of the mountain that some feel resembles Ceasar's head. The park features 7,467 preserved acres which are situated at 3,266 feet above sea level. Scenic overlook affords fantastic view of the Blue Ridge Mountain ranges. [p.11, A-5]

Croft State Park
450 Croft State Park Rd
Spartanburg, SC 29302
(803) 585-0419

7,088 acres on an old military site. Olympic-size pool, equestrian facilities, camping, boating, hiking and fishing. [p.11, A-7]

Keowee-Toxaway State Park
108 Residence Dr.
Sunset, SC 29685
(803) 868-2605
Once the center of the lower Cherokee Indian civilization, this area is rich in Indian heritage. Interpretive center features exhibits on Cherokee history. Camping and picnicking. [p.10, A-4]

Oconee State Park
624 State Park Rd
Mountain Rest, SC 29664
(803) 638-5353
This park is surrounded by Sumter National Forest and is one of the best in the state. Plenty of cabins and campsites. Swimming, boating, fishing, hiking, picnicking and carpet golf. [p.10, A-4]

Paris Mountain State Park
2401 State Park Road
Greenville, SC 29609
(803) 244-5565
Three lakes on this 1,275-acre state park provide opportunities for swimming, fishing and paddle boating (rentals). The thick forested terrain has nature and hiking trails, family camp ground, and allows for primitive camping for scout groups. [p.11, A-5]

Sadlers Creek State Park
940 Sadlers Creek Road
Anderson, SC 29624
(803) 226-8950
Water-oriented activities are very popular at this 395-acre park as well as camping (100 sites), hiking and picnicking. [p.10, B-4]

DISCOVERING

The GRAND STRAND

The Grand Strand [see map p.23] is South Carolina's premiere family vacation center. It's sixty miles of beach stretching from the North Carolina border south to Georgetown. Besides the obvious fun-in-the-sun activities, there's something for everyone here. You won't have trouble getting a tee-time at one of the 60 championship golf courses and it's unlikely that you'll return empty-handed from a day of fishing. If it happens to rain during your stay, you trip won't be ruined; there's almost as much to do inside as there is outside. Specialty shops, outlet stores, tempting seafood restaurants and arcades are open no matter what the weather brings. Myrtle Beach [p.23, E-5] is the capital of the Grand Strand, a hub of activity that will keep the brood busy from the crack of dawn 'till long after the sun goes down.

But the Atlantic Ocean is really what draws folks to the Grand Strand, and it's the reason they return. Cherry Grove, Ocean Drive, Cresent Hill, Atlantic and Windy Hill beaches dot the northern section of the Grand Strand. Surfside, Huntington and Litchfield beaches speckle the south. Myrtle Beach is in the middle with Pawley's Island and Georgetown bringing up the anchor. Each has its own special characteristics and it's a delightful challange to discover your favorite. But no matter where you plunk down your blanket you're sure to be pleased with the smell of crashing waves against the shore. Naturally, there's more to do here than merely worship

the sun. Swimming, sailing, fishing, shell collecting and simply strolling are among the more popular activities.

But the Grand Strand, and particularly Myrtle Beach, doesn't close down with the setting sun. Amusement parks and arcades are great for kids while adults and teens are inclined to do the "shag" (state dance) to the sounds of up-beat beach music. Or, if you want a break from the beach, there are diversions to satisfy almost any whim.

Golf and Tennis

It's very easy to find golf courses and tennis courts almost anywhere along the Grand Strand. Both activities are considered year-round sports in South Carolina and especially along the Grand Strand. For resort areas, greens fees are reasonable during the spring and summer and golf packages are offered throughout the year. Savvy golfers recommend visiting from mid-November through early February when the fairways are less crowded and golf plans are especially attractive. Most resorts and major hotels have their own courses but the resident pro can suggest other courses within a short driving distance. Since there are over 60 18-hole golf courses in the Grand Strand and almost 100 more throughout the state, space prevents us from providing a listing here. However, contact Myrtle Beach Golf Holiday, Box 1323, Myrtle Beach, SC 29578, (800) 845-4653. They will send you a free booklet packed with infor-

mation on each course and can provide information on accommodations and golf plans. (For more information on golfing in the Carolinas, see p.60.)

For tennis enthusiasts, the Grand Strand is a gold mine. There are almost 200 tennis courts here offering a variety of surfaces. Most are open for day and night play. Almost every hotel and resort has its own courts. Pros are available for lessons and can also direct you to other area courts. Like golf, tennis packages are offered year-round but are most economical from late fall through mid-February.

Lodging

There are over 50,000 rooms along the Grand Strand but advance reservations are required, especially during the summer months.

It's a good idea to write or call one of the following organizations. They'll be happy to send you all the information you need and to help you plan every detail of your visit to the Grand Strand.

Georgetown County Chamber of Commerce Information Center, P.O. Drawer 1776, Georgetown, SC 29442, (803) 546-8436.

Grand Strand Official Welcome Center, 2090 U.S. 501, East Conway, SC 29526, (803) 626-6619.

Myrtle Beach Area Chamber of Commerce, Box 2115, Myrtle Beach,SC 29578, (803) 626-7444 or (800) 356-3016.

Annual

FAIRS & FESTIVALS

JANUARY

Grand American Coon Hunt - Coon dogs from all over North America complete in a variety of events for cash prizes and trophies. **Orangeburg,** contact Orangeburg County Chamber of Commerce, early January, (803) 534-6821.

Oyster Festival - Sponsored by the Greater Charleston Restaurant Association, this is one of Charleston's favorite events. Aside from TONS of oysters, you'll enjoy live entertainment, crafts, exhibits, eating and recipe contests. **Charleston,** Boone Hall Plantation, late January or early February, call (803) 577-4030.

FEBRUARY

Black Heritage Tour - Driving tour encompassing the rich heritage of African Americans in the lowcountry. **Beaufort,** generally held in mid-February during Black History Month. Call (803) 522-9390 for information.

Southeastern Wildlife Eposition - Three-day celebration showcases more than $20 million in wildlife and western art including original paintings, prints, posters, sculpture, carvings and collectables. **Charleston,** mid-February, (803) 723-1748.

MARCH

Canadian-American Festival - Historical tours and sporting events welcome Canadians to the Grand Strand each March. **Myrtle Beach,** generally held in mid-month, contact Myrtle Beach Chamber of Commerce at (803) 626-7444.

Charleston Blues Festival - One of America's oldest and greatest art forms, blues music is the focus of a ten-day concert festival in historic Charleston.

Charleston, mid-March, (803) 723-1075.

Crafters Spring Classic - Extensive exhibit of woodwork, ceramic, stained glass, pottery and basket weaving. **Sumter,** Sumter County Exhibition Center, second weekend in March, call (803) 436-2270

Plantation Tours - These tours feature historically significant plantations and colonial town houses in the charming town of **Georgetown.** Generally held late March or early April, call (803) 546-8437.

APRIL

Azalea Festival - Parade, carriage rides and music celebrate the return of the azalea to the upcountry mountain region. **Pickens,** late April, call (803) 878-3258 for information.

Dogwood Festival - Spring festival featuring art and photography exhibits, music, dance and tours of historic homes. **Denmark,** first weekend in April, call (803) 793-3734 for information.

Family Circle Magazine Cup Tennis Tournament - Top seeded women compete in this highly-regarded annual event at Sea Pines Racquet Club. **Hilton Head,** late March or early April, call Sea Pines Resort (803) 785-3333.

Seafood Festival - Lowcountry seafood dishes, arts and crafts, entertainment and educational exhibits in this scenic coastal hamlet. **Murrells Inlet,** mid-April, (803) 651-2044.

South Carolina Festival of Roses - Edisto Gardens is the location of this annual event honoring the rose and featuring sports tournaments, beauty contests, live entertainment, canoe races and arts and crafts exhibits. **Orangeburg,** late April, call (803) 534-6821 for information.

Striped Bass Festival - Beside a striped bass fishing tournament, there's a parade, live entertainment and an arts and crafts show. **Manning,** early April, (803) 435-4405.

MAY

Hartscapades - Annual event to entertain the whole family features outdoor concerts, regatta, sporting events and a parade. **Hartsville,** first or second weekend in May, call (803) 332-6401 for information.

Honey Soppin' - Crafts, golf tournament, parade and a honey soppin' contest to entertain visitors. **Honea Path,** early May, call (803) 369-0555.

Mayfest - The capital city's largest arts and entertainment festival features national recording artists, art and crafts, a Southern food plaza, children's fun fair and much more. **Columbia,** early May, (803) 343-8750.

JUNE

Colonial Life Days - Participants in period costumes depict colonial life in historic Charles Towne Landing. **Charleston,** early June and early Nov., call (803) 852-4200 for information.

Hampton County Watermelon Festival - Week-long festival offers watermelon eating contests, a parade, a mud run and beauty pageant. Live entertainment. **Hampton,** late June, call (803) 943-3784 for information.

Sun Fun Festival - Several-day event featuring fireworks, beauty contest, sporting events and a gigantic castlebuilding contest. The event welcomes summer to the Grand Strand. **Myrtle Beach,** first week in June, call (803) 626-7444 for information.

JULY

Florence Family Fling - Independence day celebration

featuring ethnic foods, continuous entertainment, hot-air balloon rides and an arts and crafts show. **Florence,** July 4, call (803) 655-0515.

Harborwalk Festival - The river boardwalk is the center of activity for this festival featuring live entertainment, contests and arts and crafts exhibits. **Georgetown,** last weekend in June, call (803) 527-1688.

South Carolina Peach Festival - Ten-day event celebrates the contribution of the peach industry to South Carolina's economy. Highlights include a parade, peach fair and entertainment featuring well-known country music stars. **Gaffney,** mid-July, call (803) 489-5721 for information.

AUGUST

Carolina Craftsmen's Summer Classic - Over 230 artisans and craftsmen exhibit at this annual event in the Myrtle Beach Convention Center. **Myrtle Beach,** second or third weekend in August.

Ed Brown Rodeo - Down and dirty rodeo including trick riding, barrel racing, women's events, saddle bronc riding, bareback riding, bull riding and calf roping. **Blacksburg,** first weekend in August, call (803) 839-6239 for information.

Schuetzenfest - Ehrhardt celebrates its German heritage with German food, music, arts and crafts. **Ehrhardt,** late August, call (803) 267-5335.

South Carolina Peanut Party - This all day fun festival features tons of boiled peanuts plus road races, a bicycle race, arts and crafts, a pageant, daylong entertainment, and a carnival. **Pelion,** mid-August, (803) 734-0653.

Summerfest - An exceptional craft fair, antique and classic car show and other events help celebrate summer in **York,** late August, (803) 684-2590.

SEPTEMBER

A Taste of Charleston - An international food extravaganza with over 50 of Charleston's best restaurants giving out delicious samples. Other events include a waiters race and a beauty pageant. **Charleston,** Charles Towne Landing, late September, call (803) 557-4450 for information.

Fall House and Garden Candlelight Tour - Tours of private homes and gardens in one of Charleston's most historic districts. **Charleston,** starts late September thru October, call (803) 723-4381 for information.

Gatorade 200 and Mountain Dew Southern 500 - Both events are held at Darlington Raceway in early September. The Gatorade 200 is a Grand National Race and attracts some of the best stock car race drivers in the country. Mountain Dew Southern is known as the "granddaddy" of stock car races. **Darlington,** Labor Day weekend, call (803) 393-5931 for information.

Maritime Festival - A celebration of Charleston's maritime heritage, this festival will feature marine paintings, carvings, sculpture and other activities throughout the historic port city. **Charleston,** mid-September, (803) 221-5273.

Scottish Games and Highland Gathering - Classic Scottish games of strength and agility from the Medieval period. Bagpiping, dancers in a fair-like atmosphere. **Charleston,** mid-September, call (803) 556-2417 for information.

OCTOBER

Fall for Greenville - More than 200,000 take to the downtown streets for this food fair and its bike race, ice carving competition, soccer tournament and other events. **Greenville,** mid-October,

(803) 370-1795.

Lee County Cotton Festival - Parade, dance, road race, bed race, barbecue, carnival rides and plenty of food and live entertainment. **Bishopville,** first weekend in October, call (803) 484-5145 for information.

Oktoberfest - Festival with food, music and dancers celebrating German culture and heritage. Other activities include carnival rides, hot air ballooning and sky-diving demonstrations. **Walhalla,** third weekend in October, (803) 638-2941.

South Carolina State Fair - The state's largest and longest running fair featurs continuous live entertainment, agricultural exhibits and carnival rides. **Columbia,** 11 days in mid-October, call (803) 799-3387.

NOVEMBER

Heritage Celebration - Festival celebrating Sea Island history and culture offers crafts, exhibits, music and food. **St. Helena,** second weekend in November, call (803) 838-2432.

DECEMBER

Christmas at Hanover - Experience a colonial Christmas at Clemson University's Hanover House. **Clemson,** early December, call (803) 656-2475 for information.

Christmas at Middleton Place - Month-long holiday celebration at the mansion featuring wreathmaking, candlelight tours and special holiday dinners. December, **Charleston,** call (803) 556-6020.

Christmas Parade - Huge parade with holiday theme and all the trimmings. **Conway,** first weekend in December, call (803) 248-2273 for information.

SCENIC DRIVES
IN THE CAROLINAS

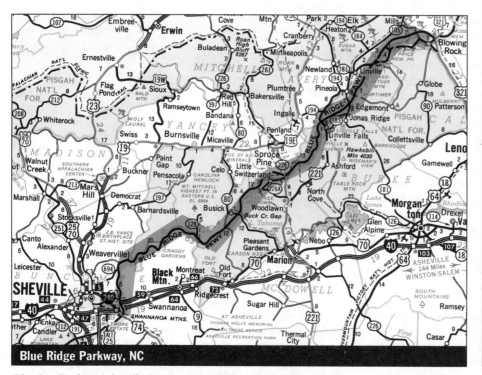

Blue Ridge Parkway, NC

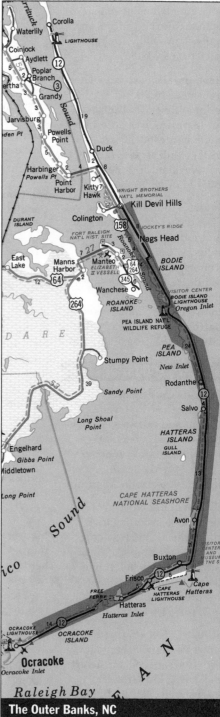

The Outer Banks, NC

Blowing Rock to Asheville (approx. 90 miles)
Over 250 miles of this scenic parkway are maintained by the National Park Service. All sections of the road are open from April 15 through November but some higher sections are closed in the event of inclement weather. The mountainous road along the summit of the Blue Ridge Parkway has numerous vistas where you can pull over and enjoy the view. Near Asheville, the parkway features hiking trails, nature centers and parks where you can stop if you tire of driving. Doughton Park is the largest recreation area along the Parkway and Linville Caverns are open for visitors to explore the stalactites and stalagmites along an underground river.

Kitty Hawk to Ocracoke (approx. 90 miles)
Along this ride you've got the Pamlico Sound on one side and the Atlantic Ocean on the other. As you drive, admire the pounding surf, the cloudless sky and the marine bird life along the seashore. You can't miss the charming port towns and fishing villages along the way. Ocracoke is especially quaint. The major attraction along this drive is the Cape Hatteras Lighthouse and the Cape Hatteras National Seashore.

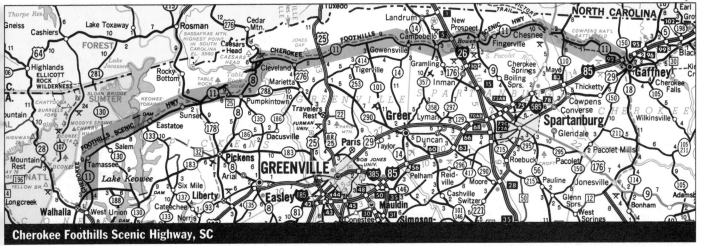

Cherokee Foothills Scenic Highway, SC

Gaffney to Walhalla (approx. 125 miles)

This road stretches for 125 miles, arcing through the mountains of South Carolina from I-85 near the North Carolina border to I-85 at the Georgia border. The foothills and rugged mountain terrain are dotted with interesting historical sights, signs for which are posted along the road. The drive is different with each season. Spring and fall are the most beautiful with blooming flowers and lush trees splashing the landscape with color.

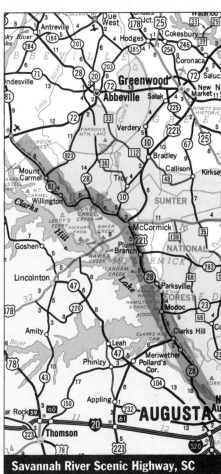

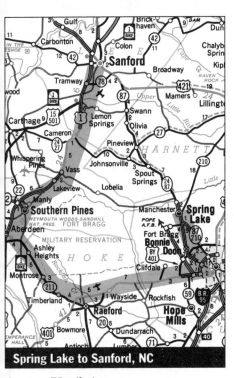

Spring Lake to Sanford, NC

Grand Strand Shoreline

Savannah River Scenic Highway, SC

(approx. 75 miles)

This ride, through the Piedmont area of North Carolina, is renowned for its panoramic beauty and top-notch recreational facilities. This is the center of North Carolina's thoroughbred horse country, a richly endowed area of stately homes and rolling green pastures. In this region, you'll find some of the state's best golf and golf resorts including the famous Pinehurst Hotel and Country Club. Also in the area is the PGA World Golf Hall of Fame.

North Myrtle Beach to Pawley's Island (approx. 60 miles)

This scenic ocean drive shows off the beautiful sea, towering dunes and the charming towns along the way. Opportunities for water sports abound and countless attractions and amusements are a short drive away. The restaurants in picturesque Murrells Inlet are famous for seafood because of the unbeatable fishing and crabbing opportunities available there. Further south is Pawley's Island, one of the oldest resorts along the Atlantic coast.

SC 28 border and SC 81 to Calhoun Falls (approx. 65 miles)

Follow the scenic highway signs for a 65-mile ride through four counties and along three major lakes. The drive is especially lovely during the spring and fall. Special attractions along this route include Calhoun Falls, Richard B. Russell Lake, Baker Creek State Park and Hickory Know State Resort Park.

THE CAROLINAS

A Golfer's Paradise

Both North and South Carolina are renowned throughout the nation for their excellent golf opportunities. All year long, visitors from all over the country, as well as Europe and Japan, flock to these two states that boast some of the nation's finest golfing. The variety of courses is as wide-ranging as the terrain: golfing along the coastal regions of South Carolina is a very different experience from golfing in the High Country of North Carolina. The natural differences in landscape and temperature, coupled with famous courses designed by legends of the game make the Carolinas a Golfer's Paradise!

GOLFING IN NORTH CAROLINA

You could golf in North Carolina every day for a year and never play the same course twice. Golf is played almost year-round in North Carolina with December and January being the least favorite months. However, mid to late February through October is open season and most visitors on a golf vacation play an average of 36 holes per day. But before you throw you clubs in the trunk and hit the road, it's a good idea to call 1-800-VISITNC. There is no golf clearinghouse or agency to give you comprehensive golf information for the state but the main tourism office in Raleigh can give you all the golf information you need for the region you plan to visit.

The Coastal Plains

Golfing in North Carolina depends largely on the state's geography. Understanding the topography, temperature and altitude of each region helps to better understand the type of golfing available there. The best known and most popular golfing in North Carolina is along the coastline from just south of Virginia Beach, Virginia to just north of Myrtle Beach, South Carolina. The inlets, bays and intracoastal waterways make for challanging, scenic courses, with white sand beaches and cool breezes creating the backdrop for the fantastic golf within residential communities and resort areas. Some of the best golf areas available along the coastal region are listed below, with information on holes/par/yardage and architect.

Bald Head Island Club, [p.14, D-2] Bald Head Island, (919) 457-5000, 18/72/6855, George Cobb

The Emerald Golf Club, [see map p.25] New Bern, (919) 636-3700; 18/72/6724, Rees Jones

Lockwood Golf Links, [p.14, D-1] Holden Beach, (919) 842-5666; 18/72/6835, Willard Byrd

The Pearl Golf Links, [p.14, D-1] Sunset Beach, (919) 579-8132; 18/72/7008, 18/72/6749, Dan Maples

Sea Trail Plantation & Golf Links, [p.14, D-1] Sunset Beach, (919) 579-4350; 18/72/6751, Dan Maples; 18/72/6761, Rees Jones; 18/72/6750, Willard Byrd

The Piedmont Plateau

The central region of North Carolina is the largest region in the state. It is also the region most densely populated with golf courses. Within it is the Sandhills, an unusual 30 mile long, 75-mile wide stretch of sand that runs throughout the middle of the state. The pleasant climate and fresh, pinescented air are other definate attractions of this golfer's mecca. The Pinehurst Resort and Country Club is the centerpiece of the golfing community of the Piedmont. Built in 1895, it boasts a total of seven courses, the most famous of which is No. 2, designed by Donald Ross, the director of Golf Generation of Pinehurst-1901-1948.

Pinehurst is also the home of the PGA/World Golf Hall of Fame, a great place to visit if you get rained out one day or have just had your fill of the links. Other resorts and residential communities in the Pinehurst area are well known for providing a variety of golf packages at every price. It's wise to call the Pinehurst Area Convention and Visitors Bureau for complete information at 1-800-346-5362. Listed on the following page are some of the Piedmont region's best golf clubs and resorts:

Duke University Golf Club, [p.26, C-4] Durham, (919) 684-2817; 18/72/7100, R.T. Jones, Sr.

Governors Club, [p.26, C-3] Chapel Hill (919) 968-8500; 18/72/7080, Jack Nicklaus

Pinehurst Resort & Country Club, [p.7, D-5] Pinehurst, (919) 295-6811 or (800) 634-9297. No.1: 18/72/5780, Donald J. Ross; No.2: 18/72/7020, Donald J. Ross; No.3: 18/71/5593, Donald J. Ross; No.4:

18/72/6919, Donald J. Ross, R.T. Jones, Rees Jones; No.5: 18/72/6827, Ellis Maples, R.T. Jones, No.6: 18/72/7157, George Fazio, Tom Fazio; No.7: 18/72/7114, Rees Jones

Tanglewood Golf Club, [p.28, B-1] Clemmons, (919) 766-0591; 18/72/7022, 18/54/1430, 18/72/6469, R.T. Jones

The High Country

Amid the breathtaking scenery of the Blue Ridge and Smoky Mountains are some of the best-and-highest-golf courses in the country.

Mountain flora and fauna go hand in hand with rocky waterfalls and majestic peaks that tantalize the senses while challenging the athlete in you. This area is rapidly becoming one of the most popular resort and vacation spots in the country with sophisticated residential communities attracting many who long to escape the scorching summer heat of the more southern states or the hustle and bustle of Northeastern cities. The availability of golf is one of the foremost attractions here and a look at what's available helps to explain why:

Cullasaja Club, [p.4, D-4] Highlands, (704) 526-9057; 18/72/6651, Arnold Palmer

Elk River Club, [p.5, B-7] Banner Elk, (704) 898-9773; 18/72/6900, Jack Nicklaus

Highlands Falls Country Club, [p.4, S-4] Highlands, (704) 526-4118; 18/70/5766, Joe Lee

Maggie Valley Resort & Country Club, [p.4, C-4] Maggie Valley, (704) 926-1616; 18/71/6300, Prevost/Bremmer

Waynesville Country Club Inn, [p.4, C-4] Waynesville, (704) 456-3551, Carolina: 9/35/2969; Blue Ridge: 9/35/2974; Dogwood: 9/35/2829. Tom Jackson

The Great Smoky Mountain Golf Association in Asheville is very helpful if you're planning a golf vacation in the mountains. Call them at (704) 258-0123.

GOLFING IN SOUTH CAROLINA

Golfing opportunities are as abundant and diverse in South Carolina as they are in North Carolina. Like its nieghbor to the north, South Carolina's golf courses, totalling over 200, are defined by their geography. Steep mountain fairways give way to woodsy rough and natural sandtraps along the shoreline. The coast of South Carolina from Myrtle Beach to Hilton Head Island is an extremely popular vacation destination and as a result has the heaviest concentration of golf courses. In fact, Myrtle Beach and Hilton Head themselves depend largely on golfers from all over the world for their revenues.

The Coastal Plains

There is really no such thing as a "bad" golf course here, although some are better than others. Many visitors just end up playing at the resort or hotel at which they are staying since most resorts have their own golf courses. However, with the exception of a few private clubs, you can play wherever you want and

enjoy not only the challenge but also the sensory pleasures of playing by the sea. To receive more information about golfing along the coast in South Carolina you should call the following organizations: Myrtle Beach Chamber of Commerce, (800) 356-3016; Hilton Head Island Chamber of Commerce, (803) 785-3673. Also, the South Carolina Department of Parks, Recreation and Tourism in Columbia can send you a map of the state with each course listed by region giving holes, par, length and telephone. Call (803) 734-0122 for your copy.

Sea Pines Resort, Hilton Head (800) 845-6131; 18/71/6850, Pete Dye and Jack Nicklaus [see map p.25]

Wild Dunes Links, [p.19, E-8] Isle of Palms, (803) 886-6000; 18/72/6800, 18/70/6400, Tom Fazio

Heritage Club, [p.17, A-8] Pawley's Island, (803) 626-3887; 18/71/7100, Larry Young

Myrtle Beach National Golf Club, [p.13, D-7] Myrtle Beach (800) 344-5590; 18/72/6900 (West), Frank Duane, Arnold Palmer

Possum Trot Golf Club, [p.13, D-8] North Myrtle Beach, (800) 626-8768; 18/72/6966, Russell Breeden

The Piedmont

The central area of South Carolina is loaded with huge oaks and sandy tracks of land and is generously dotted with lakes and streams. The mild winters and challenging terrain are very alluring to golfers of all abilities. This is also well-known as thoroughbred country, where wealthy capitalists from the Northeast years ago decided to winter and raise their horses. Today, golf courses abound. Some are private but many more are open to the public.

Santee-Cooper Country Club, [p.17, A-5] Santee, (800) 344-6534; 18/72/6615, Eddie Riccobonni

Country Club of South Carolina, [p.13, C-5] Florence, (803) 669-0920; 18/72/7200, Ellis Maples

Cooper's Creek Golf Club, [p.12, D-1] Pelion, (803) 894-3666; 18/72/6550, Red Chase

Midland Valley Country Club, [p.18, E-4] Aiken, (803) 663-7332; 18/71/6870, Ellis Maples

Upcountry South Carolina

Golfing in the Upcountry region of South Carolina offers some diversity as well. Aside from the rocky scenery, the balmy weather provides ideal conditions for golf, with temperatures in the mid-80s in the summer and falling only to the mid-40s in the coldest months of the year. There are many well-groomed public courses and it is best to call Discover Upcountry Carolina Association at (803) 233-2690 for more specific information. But wherever you go, you are sure to find a challenge as well as a feast for the senses in the steep mountain terrain of this area.

Bonnie Brae Golf Club, [p.11, A-5] Greenville, (803) 277-9838; 18/72/6575

Cotton Creek Golf Club, [p.11, A-7] Spartanburg, (803) 583-7084; 18/72/6653

Oconee Country Club, [p.10, B-4] Seneca, (803) 882-8037; 18/71/6100

Southern Oaks, [p.11, A-5] Powdersville, (803) 859-6698; 18/72/6710, Willie B. Lewis

Table Rock Resort [p.11, A-5] Pickens, (803) 878-2030; 18/72/6500

For two relatively small states, the Carolinas contain a disproportionately high number of nationally designated parks, forest and seashores. North Carolina alone contains one national park, two national  seashores and four national forests while South Carolina boasts two national forests. What follows is a description of the most scenic National Park Service areas in both Carolinas. ✺

NATIONAL PARKS

⚙ North Carolina

CAPE HATTERAS NATIONAL SEASHORE [p.9, C-8] is the narrow, broken stretch of barrier islands that curve out into the Atlantic Ocean and back again as a protective arm are along North Carolina's mainland. The strand of islands is 70 miles long and is commonly called the Outer Banks. The islands, Bodie, Hatteras and Ocracoke, are connected by State Highway 12 and the Hatteras Inlet Ferry. The shallow waters of Pamlico Sound [p.9, D-7] are bordered by the North Carolina mainland to the west and the Outer Banks to the east. Here, land and sea mesh to form offshore sanctuaries, a haven for many species of birds, plants and sea animals. The stretch of beaches, dunes, marshes and woodlands have survived the wild impulses of Mother Nature and the omnipresent power of the sea. Fiercely guarded by the U.S. Department of the Interior, Cape Hatteras is a special place of wonderment and discovery.

All types of bird life populate the shores year-round. Visitors to Cape Hatteras National Seashore are often joined by flocks of migrating geese or persnickety shore birds searching for food. Fishermen are routinely delighted with the fishing off the Outer Banks. Trout, bass, blue fish, tuna and the occasional marlin come in with the tide and occupy experienced anglers and weekend warriors for hours at a time. Those less patient can often fill a bucket with clams and crabs just by strolling along the beach. When the shore is peaceful and without the threat of impending gale winds, recreational opportunities abound; sailing, surfing, swimming and sunbathing are among the most popular.

Alas, the sea is not always so kind and the perilous waters off the coast are called the "Graveyard of the Atlantic." A disturbing, yet accurate handle, the Graveyard has claimed over 600 ships and many more lives in the past 400 years. Today the Coast Guard patrols these waters meticulously and there are few shipwrecks, but ruins of previous wrecks will probably be uncovered for decades to come. For obvious reasons, each island has its own lighthouse. The most famous, Cape Hatteras Lighthouse, [p.9, D-8] was built in 1870 and, at 208 feet, is the tallest in the United States.

For more information contact: Superintendent, Cape Hatteras National Seashore, Rt 1, Box 675, Manteo, NC 27954 (919) 473-2111.

CAPE LOOKOUT NATIONAL SEASHORE [p.15, A-6] is also on the Outer Banks of North Carolina and extends 55 miles south from Ocracoke Island. There are no roads or bridges to these unspoiled barrier islands and access is possible only by boat. The seashore is completely undeveloped and there are no maintained roads. The isolation of the wide, bare beaches and constantly shifting dunes provide a peaceful retreat for visitors.

If, however, you're looking for more than the bare-bones Robinson Crusoe experience, don't despair. Fishing, boating, camping and hiking are all popular and permitted activities on Cape Lookout. Since there are no rentals available, all recreational boating is done with personal boats. However, chartered boats and ferries are available both to and from the island. Boats, both power and sail, are used for access, sight-seeing and fishing. You don't need a boat to fish, though. The surf fishing here is among the best on the Atlantic Coast–just don't forget your hip boots in the fall when the waters are most plentiful.

Camping on Cape Lookout is challenging, exciting and primitive. If you can't go a day without using a blowdyer, running water or other by-products of RV hookups, better think twice before camping here. There are no developed campsites, few shady spots and no concessions for supplies, food or drink. Unless you're a Green Beret or a pushover for survival courses make sure you bring everything you need from drinking water to extra-long stakes to secure tents in the sand. Hikers and day-trippers should also be well prepared. However, don't be discouraged from visiting Cape Lookout; the miles of naked beach primed for swimming, sunning, crabbing and beach-combing are an unparalleled delight. So prepare to meet nature on her own terms. With careful planning and attention to detail, a visit to Cape Lookout can be an unforgettable experience.

For more information contact: Superintendent, Cape Lookout National Seashore, 131 Charles St., Island, NC 28531 (919) 728-2250.

THE GREAT SMOKY MOUNTAINS NATIONAL PARK [see map p.22] offers 514,093 acres of wilderness and is the country's most popular National Park. Half in

Tennessee and half in North Carolina, the park is the apex of the Appalachian Highlands. It gets its name from the smoke-like haze cloaking the majestic mountain tops as they reach heavenward. The virgin forests, fertile soils and abundance of plants and flowers never fail to entrance visitors.

Each season in the Smokies brings a rich variety of colors, sights and sound to mesmerize the senses. In winter a blanket of peace covers the region. Birds have migrated, many animals have hibernated and white fog envelops frost covered peaks blurring the difference between the two. In spring and summer the variety of wildlife and flora provide a panorama of nature study. Bright flowers carpet the forest floor and blooming rhododendrons flood the surroundings in color. Startled deer leap gracefully from tree to tree hiding from excited visitors while roaring bears inspire the same feeling in humans. Fall is a spectacular pageant of color and light with ideal climate conditions making it the optimal season for sightseeing and hiking.

Historic structures dot the park's landscape and help tell the story of these mountains. The Appalachian Trail [p.22, E-2] extends 70 miles along the state line between North Carolina and Tennessee. Nearby, restored historic log cabins and barns serve as remembrances of the English and Scottish pioneers who left their homeland to start new lives in the wilderness. Evidence of the fallen Cherokee Nation is also here. Cherokees hid in these mountains in the winter of 1838-39 before being driven cruelly along the Trail of Tears into Oklahoma.

The park has been preserved for the dual purpose of protecting the wildlife and environment while allowing visitors the chance to enjoy the scenic beauty and rich heritage of this part of the country. There is ample opportunity for hiking, camping and fishing at designated areas throughout the park. Nature walks and other naturalist activities are offered during the summer. The aesthetics of the park provide a fantastic blend of lush wildlands and an outdoor tribute to pioneer life. Visitors are urged to experience both.

For more information contact: Superintendent, Great Smoky Mountains National Park, 107 Park Headquarters Road, Gatlinburg, TN 37738, (615) 436-1200.

South Carolina

FRANCIS MARION NATIONAL FOREST [p.17, A-6] is comprised of nearly 250,000 acres of wildlife and wilderness in the Coastal Plains near Charleston. Early colonial settlements are preserved within an area thick with pine, moss-hung oaks and flowering trees. It was here during the Revolutionary War that General Francis Marion battled against Colonel Banastre Tarleton's British troops, [Marion is buried at Belle Isle, his family's plantation near Eadytown]. The small lakes that dot the forest are thought to have been formed by fallen meteors and provide ample opportunity for fishing, swimming and boating. Camping, hiking, horseback riding and hunting are permitted.

SUMTER NATIONAL FOREST [p.10, A-4] is located in the Piedmont Plateau. The miles of trails throughout the 250,000-acre tract seem endless. The pine and hardwood forest is not only lovely to behold but also provides ideal conditions for hunting quail, deer and turkey. Shotguns, rifles and bows and arrows are permitted. The rivers that run through the forest allow canoeing, swimming and fishing.

For information on both of these National Forests contact: National Forest Service, 1835 Assembly St., Rm. 333, Columbia, SC 29201, (803) 765-5222.

NOTE: *Before hunting or fishing in North Carolina check with the Wildlife Resources Commission Archdale Building 512 N. Salisbury St. Raleigh, NC 27604-1188 (919) 733-3391.*

In South Carolina write or call: Wildlife and Marine Resources Department P.O. Box 167 Columbia, SC 29202 (803) 734-3888

Both organizations will furnish information on seasons, regulations, licensing and fees.